M000026132

Waiting
on
HEAVEN

Waiting on HEAVEN

VICTORIA MASON ACREE

PLAIN SIGHT PUBLISHING
AN IMPRINT OF CEDAR FORT, INC.
SPRINGVILLE, UT

ISBN 13: 978-1-4621-1399-6

Published by Plain Sight Publishing, an imprint of Cedar Fort, Inc.
2373 W. 700 S., Springville, UT 84663
Distributed by Cedar Fort, Inc., www.cedarfort.com

LIBRARY OF CONGRESS CATALOGING-IN-PUBLICATION DATA

Acree, Victoria Mason, 1956- author.
Waiting on heaven / Victoria Mason Acree.
    pages cm
Summary: A mother has an out-of-body experience following the death of her ten-year-old daughter Paris Pardue Acree.
ISBN 978-1-4621-1399-6
1. Terminally ill children. 2. Terminal care--Psychological aspects. 3. Mother and child. 4. Mothers and daughters. 5. Acree, Paris Pardue, 1990-2001--Health. 6. Children--Death. I. Title.

RJ249.A27 2013
362.17'5083--dc23

2013033360

Cover design by Angela D. Baxter
Cover design © 2014 by Lyle Mortimer
Edited and typeset by Whitney Lindsley

Printed in the United States of America

10 9 8 7 6 5 4 3 2 1

Printed on acid-free paper

TO THE MEMORY OF
MY DAUGHTER AND TEACHER

Paris Pardue Acree

DECEMBER 23, 1990–FEBRUARY 15, 2001

The journal entry that Paris Pardue Acree wrote in December of 2000, two months before she died of brain-stem cancer.

December 11, 2000
How I love you, I can't explain.
I'm like a rose, already bloomed
and ready to sing.
Though I love you, I have to go.
Heavenly Father is calling
me home.

By Paris P. Acree
To Mummy

A MOTHER'S VERSE TO HER DAUGHTER

Birth brings forth your rosy face,
Nine hours labor, time well spent.
Cupped in hands that frame with grace,
Starting out to enjoy life's rent.
Life with happy smile, birthdays ten,
Ballet classes, and Girl Scouts too.
Love of school, love of paper and pen,
Joy of family, disappointments few.
Death so soon! Your years are numbered short,
My joy, my love, never to be eleven,
But blessed with time to say "Bye" of a sort
As you now take your walk through heaven.
Remember me, do not forget me! To me you said.
Oh no, my Paris, together again we will be one day.

Victoria Mason Acree (Mummy), 2001

CONTENTS

PROLOGUE

Many would-be authors begin their writing journey by brainstorming ideas for the perfect title and content for the perfect book, hoping to write something meaningful, informative, or entertaining. This was not the case in my experience. For me, there was no research to be done, no reference books to check out, and no input required from others. For me, the words came through me, straight from a place beyond the heart, and, more important, from a realm of another state of consciousness, from the true essence of a little girl who was known as Paris Pardue Acree.

It was July 2012, and I was still awakening from the motion of sitting up in my bed in the dark.

"What am I doing back here?"

I spoke the words out loud. I looked around the room and saw that I was sitting up in my own bed, surrounded by my own bedroom furniture, in my own bedroom, in my own house.

"Where else would I expect to be . . ." I looked at the clock on my nightstand. ". . . at 3:21 in the morning?"

I jumped up out of my bed and rushed with enthusiasm to my little home office. I squeezed through several packing boxes that would be loaded onto a moving truck the next week as I relocated to the Wasatch Mountains of Utah. I didn't quite know why I needed to move there, but I was following a strong inner prompting. I grabbed hold of a yellow legal pad and a pen and rushed back to my bedroom, jumping on my bed like a giddy teenager. It was there, with a feeling of great enthusiasm and excitement, that I began writing a list. The list was of the many experiences I'd

1

had with my late daughter, Paris Pardue Acree, who had died of brain stem cancer at the age of ten, eleven years before, in 2001.

The list started with my own out-of-body experience, after Paris's memorial service. Next on the list was the shared death experience with her upon her death. My pen kept going, and the list continued with the many things that Paris had shared with me, including telling me that I had breast cancer just two weeks after she was diagnosed with an astrocytoma in her brain stem.

This list read like a shopping list or a to-do list, sometimes using a single word or a short phrase. I sat and looked at the list that just seemed to flow out of my pen. Then, the flow continued going back further, more words and phrases, back to the day I realized I was pregnant with Paris. Tired and weary, and with little to no thought at all, I lay down and went back to sleep.

It was midmorning, and I was awake again, sitting up in bed, when I saw the yellow legal pad lying on the bed beside me. I recalled writing "the list" during the night. I sat for a while just looking at the list. Instantly I felt a big smile on my face, and I began to laugh out loud; bursts of smiling and laughing out loud had become regular experiences for me since acquiring an almost continued sixth sense, a higher state of consciousness, or "Knowingness" since my return after my out-of-body experience. I knew in that instant that the list I was looking at were the chapters of a book—this book.

—Victoria Mason Acree

Chapter 1

THE CONCEPTION
OF AN ANGEL

Nursing my newborn baby girl, Helen, was always a delight. I would often think to myself that it would be so nice for her to have a little brother or sister to play with sometime down the road. Nursing every two hours around the clock, pretty much ensured, or so I thought, that falling pregnant again would be quite unlikely, and no birth control was used because another baby would be dearly welcomed into our family . . . sometime down the road.

Taking care of my now-four-month-old Helen and our active family, I found myself feeling a little more tired than usual. Still nursing Helen resulted in irregular and often missed menstruation, and I totally missed those first tell-tale signs of tender breasts of a new pregnancy.

My pregnancy was confirmed on the March 28, on my thirty-fourth birthday. What a wonderful birthday present that was for me, and how delighted the family was that another baby was on the way. Helen was to have a baby brother or sister, a playmate, sooner rather than later. My due date was December 29, 1990, a belated Christmas gift for all the family.

My first twenty weeks of pregnancy went like clockwork. Apart from feeling tired, I kept well and once again felt those wondrous feelings of a new life growing inside me. How I loved those late evening hours when I could just lie back and caress my unborn baby as it turned inside me. What would it be, a boy or a girl? I didn't care one way or the other—I just wanted it to be healthy.

It was always exciting for me to visit my obstetrician's office. Listening to that precious little heartbeat was a great joy to my ears. Often I would feel my own heart flutter, almost in acknowledgment of the beating heart of the new life that appeared on the screen of the ultrasound monitor. All seemed to be going well with the baby's development, but the obstetrician did want to do a blood test to check for any possibility of spina bifida as I was thirty-four years old and from the United Kingdom, where spina bifida is said to be more common in the babies of women my age. The blood was drawn, and I left my obstetrician's office feeling confident that all was well with my baby; it was just a test after all.

At home, life was a little hectic. By now my milk had changed to match my pregnancy, and it was no longer satisfying to Helen; her weaning from me to formula happened quite naturally. While I missed that closeness of nursing her, it did allow for other family members to bottle-feed her and share that wonderful experience of a baby happily feeding.

Thinking ahead, I wondered how I was going to cope with a newborn and a thirteen-month-old and two growing teens. However, I knew that the love of a mother would always find a way.

Chapter 2

LOVED, NO MATTER WHAT

Busy with the demands of the day and what seemed like endless chores, it was often a relief for the phone to ring. It was a good excuse to sit at the kitchen table and chat with a friend. Of course, it was all baby talk since many of my friends were pregnant too. I didn't know the gender of the baby yet because he or she never did make the gender obvious at any of the ultrasound appointments. It didn't really matter—all I wanted was a healthy baby—but I did think it would be nice to have another little girl as a playmate for Helen, and initially we would also save so much money on baby clothes since Helen was growing out of her tiny clothes so quickly and they still looked like new. Then again, it would be nice to have another boy because my eldest son was now a teenager, and hugging and kissing his mother was no longer kosher at his age, or so he thought anyway. There would be just thirteen months between my babies, and I knew I would be busier than ever before, but it would be a wonderful way to be busy. I so loved babies, especially my own.

This particular phone call was from my obstetrician's office. The test result for spina bifida was in, and I was asked to make an appointment as soon as possible because the doctor would like to share the results with me immediately. Make the appointment as soon as possible, immediately? I asked the receptionist if everything was okay with my baby. Of course, this was a stupid question to ask the receptionist. She wouldn't know, and if she did, she would not be allowed to tell me, and not on the phone. I was starting to feel anxious and just wanted to know what the result was and the feelings of panic were settling in my chest.

No, there is no way my baby has spina bifida! That was something that happened in other families, not mine! I didn't sleep a wink that night. I took solace in the night sky over Albuquerque, New Mexico, as I sat on the back porch most of the night while the rest of the family slept. I searched the sky, counting the stars and asking God for enough strength to get me through the night. I took it for granted that I would have a healthy child. I caressed my unborn baby as it turned inside me, wrapping the blanket around my tummy to keep my baby warm.

I recalled the painful episodes in my younger years. I had been raised in the hell of domestic violence, with a sexually abusive father, a mother who constantly reminded me that she should have gotten rid of me, and, worst of all, I had endured the painful experience of my older brother's suicide. These events were stuffed down again and again—I always meant to deal with them but left it to "someday." As the starry night gave way to a beautiful sunrise over the Sandia Mountains, I cried thinking of the challenges that may be ahead and how it may impact the whole family. I'd had more than my share of past sorrow; surely God wouldn't let harm come to my unborn child.

Then I pulled myself together with the realization that I had not met with the doctor yet and that I may well be getting all upset over nothing at all. I consoled myself the rest of the morning with the thought that I was just being emotional, as pregnant women often are. *No matter what the doctor tells me, my baby is loved, no matter what.*

My appointment time came and went, and the longer I sat in the waiting room, the more anxiety was tightening in my chest. After a while, which seemed like forever, I was met by my doctor, who smiled a reassuring smile, but I could sense that his smile was covering up some bad news. I already started to feel relief just hearing my name being called.

The obstetrician started,

"The result of the spina bifida test is in, and I'm pleased to inform you that the count is so low that we can rule out spina bifida."

I started to cry with relief, and it felt like a weight had been lifted off my chest, and I could breathe easier.

The doctor continued, "But, with numbers so very low, I need to make you aware that there is a strong likelihood that your baby may have Down syndrome."

My head was reeling. *Down syndrome, is that what he said to me? Did I hear him right?* I went from feeling elated at the negative result for spina bifida to feeling nauseated from a pit in my stomach. I started to cry—my emotions were on a roller coaster, and I couldn't control them.

At twenty weeks of my pregnancy, my obstetrician continued, "The only way to know for sure if your baby is Down syndrome is to have an amniocentesis, but . . ."

Here we go again.

". . . to do so at this stage of your pregnancy, there would be a slight possibility of a spontaneous abortion. The possibility is low, but I need to inform you of the risk. Then you can make a decision on how you would want to proceed should the result be positive."

I was shaking and wanted to throw up.

"No! There is no way I will risk losing my baby. He or she is already so loved and wanted, no matter what."

After some lengthy questions and answers with the doctor, I was gripped with fear when he asked,

"Is there any history of Down syndrome in your family?"

Oh, God, yes there was.

"Yes, my father's cousin, my second cousin."

I remembered Patsy from my childhood. His condition was severe, I recalled. He died at the age of forty-one. He had been very dependent on his family all his life. I remembered also as a child being a little afraid of him. He loved to be physically playful. He never meant any harm; he just didn't know his own strength.

The doctor's office required me to sign a few forms stating that the test result had been fully explained to me and that I understood the explanations including the recommendation for an amniocentesis, including the possible risk of a spontaneous abortion, which I declined. I signed the papers, digging the point of the pen into the paper with feelings of resentment. I didn't know to whom or what I was resentful, but it was a foreboding feeling.

I left the doctor's office in tears, holding my baby bump as if to protect it from the impending syndrome. Determined to be strong, I tried to stay focused on taking care of my family. I stopped at the local grocery store on my way back from my obstetrician's office to do the weekly grocery shopping. I badly needed a distraction at this point, and as much as grocery shopping was a chore for me, I found some relief by being in a crowd. There I felt normal, just like everyone else in the store.

Rounding the frozen food aisle, I bumped my shopping cart into another customer's. She was a younger woman with a small child who was sitting in her shopping cart. I gasped as I saw that the little boy had Down syndrome. I panicked, and the mother must have notice my reaction. I abandoned my shopping cart and headed for the door and ran across the parking lot as if to take shelter from my fears by climbing into my car and locking the door.

The reality of what I had just done scared me. What must've that young mother thought of me? Did she think I was disgusted at the appearance of her Down syndrome child? Should I go back in the store and find her and apologize for my behavior? How could I explain the fear and dread that was cutting through me like a sharp knife? I didn't have the guts to go back into the store. I took a few minutes to compose myself and make the short drive home.

While I loved my family dearly, our home was always a hive of activity; endless questions on endless topics. "Mum" this, and "Mum" that. I was either the angel or the witch depending on what hormone was kicking in at any given moment. I wanted to be alone with my thoughts, and the bathroom became my sanctuary. I had another twenty weeks to go with my pregnancy; the baby was due the week after Christmas. This would be a long twenty weeks. The uncertainty was the most painful. If only I could know for sure, then I could prepare myself. The amniocentesis was the only way to know for sure, but I was not willing to risk a spontaneous abortion.

We attended church each Sunday, and after the service I would escape to my bedroom as the family gave me the rest of the day off after I cooked dinner. All I could do was pray. I prayed morning, noon, and night. I prayed when I was driving, and I prayed when I was doing the laundry, and I prayed in the shower. *Does God even listen to me? Can he hear me?*

I often sat watching the night sky and recalling my childhood and the fond memories of Patsy, my second cousin with Down syndrome, and how his mother, Auntie Bette, loved him. He was an only child and took up all of Auntie Bette's time. He was a handful, but I remember him as always laughing. He was always happy when others were not. This gave me comfort, to think that my child would be happy, no matter what. But I was plagued with thoughts of who was going to take care of my child when I was too old or dead. Would Helen be willing to be a caregiver for her Down syndrome sibling? The answers hurt too much to consider them any further. I just surrendered all my fears and focused on the one thing that I did know: I loved my baby, no matter what.

I was determined to be as prepared as possible for my baby coming into this world. I spent many afternoons in the local bookstore, picking up one book after another on the subject of parenting a Down syndrome child. Thankfully Helen was a good baby, and she napped in her stroller as I read. None of the books I read gave me any relief; one thing was obvious to me, and that was it would be a big adjustment for the whole family. It was more than just me educating myself on the subject. How would my older kids handle this? What do I tell them? Do I bring up the subject now, just in case, or do I leave it and wait? The waiting and all the uncertainty was the hardest part.

Chapter 3

HOPING FOR THE BEST, PREPARING
FOR THE WORST

The last twenty weeks of my pregnancy were coming to an end. Although it would be Helen's second Christmas, it would be the first that I would see the excitement in her little eyes as she was now old enough to play with her new toys. But the excitement was tinged with sadness. I was getting myself as prepared as I could, yet the diagnosis had not been confirmed, but with those "very low numbers" and cousin Patsy, I felt that there was a strong likelihood that the baby would be born with Down syndrome. The phrase "very low number" had been my silent mantra for almost twenty weeks, like a demon in my head.

It seemed as if every place I went I saw Down syndrome kids—in stores, at church, and even at our Wednesday afternoon visits to the zoo that Helen loved so much. I couldn't do anything but wait. I went through some self-pity. It was like a dice was being rolled or Russian roulette. Spina bifida was ruled out. Now possibly Down syndrome?

In the last month before the birth, I was diagnosed with gestational diabetes, and this diagnosis was definite. My blood sugar was off the chart, and the condition was bad enough that I was given a prescription and instructions to give myself insulin shots daily. *My poor little baby, what else can we be diagnosed with—and you're not even born yet. Hang in there, baby. Mummy loves you no matter what!*

We had decorated the house for Christmas and made sure that Santa Claus would give everyone in the family most of the items on their "Dear Santa" letters. I just had one wish for Christmas . . . that I just get to hold my baby safely in my arms. I guess I got tired of worrying; I felt worn out. It didn't matter anymore, no matter what.

It was two days before Christmas Eve, while shopping in a toy store, that I saw a male customer behave in a manner that upset me, and, right then and there, I felt the *pop* of my water breaking and realized that I was in labor. At last the long wait would be over.

The doctor had told me that the most accurate method in identifying Down syndrome in a newborn was by taking a cross-section of the umbilical cord to the laboratory. The presence of an "extra" cord within the umbilical cord would confirm the diagnosis. Likewise, the absence of the "extra" cord would rule out Down syndrome with certainty. We had secured having a neonatologist present at the delivery to take immediate care of my baby.

I had been in labor for twenty-four hours, but I stayed home for most of that time. It was now Sunday afternoon, and I decided to knit a little girl's bonnet to match the little coat that I had knitted the week before; I loved knitting baby clothes. We still had not chosen a name for sure, but there was a coffee advertisement on the television all afternoon, and it was for a French roast coffee from Paris. We had already decided that Pardue would be included in a baby's name after a paternal great-grandmother who was dearly loved and who passed away many years earlier. So while knitting and listening to the coffee advertisement and the name Paris all afternoon, it was settled. If the baby was a little girl, her name would be Paris Pardue Acree, and Luke Bernard Mason Acree after my late brother for a little boy.

After laboring all day, we left for the hospital around 10:00 p.m. The gestational diabetes had taken its toll on my little one. While I had delivered three babies previously quite naturally, it soon became obvious that the baby had become stuck in the birth canal. No amount of pushing was bringing about the delivery. The forceps that were used were not helping either. The last ultrasound showed that the baby was larger on the upper half of its body than on the lower half of the body, with heavy shoulders. In other words, the baby was proportioned in a way that would make the delivery a harder push. Delivery by cesarean section would have been best for both the baby and me, but it was no longer an option at this late stage of labor. The nurse turned the baby's monitor off; this was not a good sign for me, and I was starting to panic. The doctor then appeared in front of my face and told me straight,

"This baby has to come out on the next push, do you understand me?"

The look on the doctor's face matched what I was feeling inside. The nurse had turned off the baby's heart monitor, on which I could once hear the little racing heartbeat slow down and become faint. *Please, God, bring my baby into this world alive.* Exhausted as I was, that energy to push harder, and sustain it, showed up from who knows where. I could feel my body tearing as my baby came into the world at 11:01 p.m.

Chapter 4

HAPPY BIRTHDAY, PARIS PARDUE ACREE!

*I*t's a girl! But no crying! My newborn baby girl, my little Paris, was alive but needed oxygen. The neonatologist took her and stimulated her. Her birth had been traumatic for her as her body had become stuck in the birth canal and she experienced being crushed. I soon heard her cry, and I cried too with relief. I was so relieved that she was born alive that I had forgotten all my worry over the possibility that she may have Down syndrome.

As I lay there trying to relax a little, Paris had been taken out of the delivery room by the neonatologist. I knew that they were checking her for possible birth injuries and to take a sample of her cord to check for Down syndrome. It was only thirty minutes, but it seemed like an eternity. The doctor came back into the room with a big smile on her face and the baby wrapped in a pink blanket. Walking toward me, she asked, "Do you have a name for your baby girl?"

"Yes, her name is Paris, Paris Pardue Acree."

The doctor put Paris in my arms, and I held her so tight that she cried.

"Paris has no Down syndrome as no 'extra' cord was present in the umbilical cord, but she is badly bruised on her nose, cheekbones, and her shoulders, so she has to be handled very gently."

I was at a loss for words; all that worry for four and a half months, and she was okay. Paris was by far my largest baby at eight pounds, three ounces; Helen had been six pounds, three ounces. I had a small frame, and it felt like delivering a ten-pound baby. The gestational diabetes caused Paris to be top heavy, and the greatest weight was on her upper body. By the time the nurses and doctors took care of both Paris and me, it was late. The doctor said she wanted to keep Paris in the neonatal care unit until morning since she had been quite traumatized by her birth, and they wanted to monitor her closely.

I slept the rest of the night, and in the morning Paris was brought to me, and I was told that she may cry some and to handle her very gently. Paris had very bruised shoulders and a swollen face and was in a lot of physical pain. Poor baby, she had quite a painful journey into this world, but no spina bifida and no Down syndrome.

I held Paris as gently as I could and smiled at this new little baby girl that had come into my life, and the feelings of love for her just flowed. Later that morning, the family came to see their new baby sister. Helen looked so big next to Paris; Helen was so tender with Paris quite naturally, almost as if she knew her pain. It was a sweet sight.

Paris was only twelve hours old when the doctor gave the all clear to take her home that Christmas Eve morning. I was so excited! I couldn't wait to see Helen again; I missed her so much! This was going to be a special Christmas.

We had not expected Paris to be born before Christmas, so we hadn't bought any Christmas presents for her. The family went Christmas shopping to buy gifts for her, and I stayed home with Paris by myself. I laid her in her bassinet and knelt down beside her and thanked God for her and that she was healthy. I knew in time her bruises and her physical pain would go away and her body weight would balance out. The family came home with many cuddly toys for her. I think Santa would agree that Paris had been a good little girl, and a soft cuddly dolly would be under the tree for her.

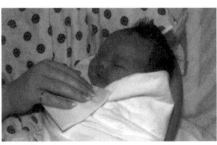

Newborn Paris

Chapter 5

PARIS'S FIRST CHRISTMAS

Since Paris was born a week earlier than her due date, friends were making a last-minute dash to the store to make sure that she would have gifts under the Christmas tree. The best part of that Christmas Day was watching Helen looking intensely at baby Paris. Out of all the toys and dollies that Helen got that morning, this little bundle called Paris made the most noise. At one point, while Paris was lying on a blanket on the floor, Helen took her dolly, which was longer than Paris, by the leg and dragged it along the floor to her toy box. Then she came back to Paris and took her by the leg also and tried to drag her across the floor to the toy box too. Helen really thought that Paris was another dolly. Paris and Helen wore matching red velvet dresses that Christmas Day. That was a happy Christmas for the most part, blighted only by the absence of my eldest child, my only son. All the worry of spina bifida and Down syndrome was past now, and it seemed that all that was ahead was a fun-filled childhood for these two little sisters.

Chapter 6

THE FORMATIVE YEARS

*D*espite being a little over eight pounds at birth, Paris was a petite child, but she was as quick as a whippet and always was trying her best to keep up with Helen. Being thirteen months older than Paris, Helen naturally hit all those first milestones ahead of Paris. I remember well Paris's frustration at pumping her legs on the swing by herself. She would just stare at Helen in amazement at how she managed to get that swing to go higher and higher. Paris studied her sister's movement until it dawned on her how to move her body, and once she got it, she got it!

Paris was mature for her age, especially in her speech and communication skills. I taught both the girls to read phonetically at an early age, and they both were reading simple books before their third birthdays. Reading became a favorite pastime for them both. Among the other activities Paris enjoyed were ballet and tap dance. She was so little, and, with those little feet tapping on any hard surface, she was a joy to watch. Gymnastics was another activity she enjoyed; she could hurl her little body around those bars so fast that it scared me. I withdrew her from gymnastics because I was afraid that at some point she would come flying off the apparatus and hurt herself, possibly permanently. Paris had no fear, but I did. Girls Scouts was another one of her favorite things to participate in, especially when it came time to sell those Girl Scout cookies—she expected me to buy every box them.

Over the next few years, our family enjoyed the diversity of living in Colorado and, in 1994, settling in Austin, Texas. Then in 1996 we rented out our family home and spent a year in a small principality in the

Paris eating a "Paris bun"

Paris and Helen at South Padre Island

northern mountains of Japan. Paris and Helen loved the time they spent there. Being just five years old at the time, Paris picked up enough Japanese to communicate with the Japanese children in the neighborhood where we lived. Travel was another big hit with her, and she loved visiting my native Scotland, where the bakers' shops sold "Paris buns," almost like little pointed muffins with sugar sprinkles on top. She enjoyed the beaches of Cancun, Mexico, and the island of Oahu, but most of all she loved South Padre Island, a sandbank off the southern coast of Texas and out in the Gulf of Mexico. There she played in the froggy pool with Helen at the beautiful Sheraton Hotel. Hers really was a charmed, happy life.

Chapter 7

PARIS: THE PUPIL
AND THE TEACHER

When not at home, Paris loved to be in school—or possibly she preferred school to home. Learning was exciting to her, and she appeared to learn any subject quite effortlessly. Straight As were less common than the A-pluses on her report cards. Reading was by far her greatest love, and she tested out at a twelfth-grade reading level while in the fourth grade.

While Paris behaved typically for her age, she would shine brightly at times. Her teacher would tell me about these brighter episodes when they happened at school. On more than one occasion, when fighting broke out in the schoolyard, Paris was called for by the young bystanders. Paris would be seen to give a lecture to the quarrelsome duos and point out that they were really brothers and to not be unkind to each other. She just had a way about her that attracted others, including adults. For a young child, she had an uncanny wisdom about her; more than one teacher had described her as "an old soul." It was during the early part of her fourth-grade class that Paris befriended a little boy, Tom, who was labeled with attention deficit hyperactive disorder (ADHD). Paris made it her mission to help him as best she could. She would finish her classroom assignments quickly and then would be there at Tom's side. She assured her teacher she would not give Tom the answers but would help him to understand the questions. Tom was not the most popular child in class because, more often than not, his behavior was a distraction to other students. Paris had a soft spot for Tom and often said she could feel his sadness.

"He is sad inside, Mummy," she would say as she gave her report of the day at the dinner table. Over time, Paris became known as "Tom's teacher." Paris liked that a lot!

"There is nothing wrong with Tom, Mummy. He just learns differently than the other kids, that's all," she would say in a strong matter-of-fact way. Paris had great patience with "her student," Tom. Tom took a liking to Paris, and he responded with some of the best class work he had ever done. There was an occasion at one of Paris's parent-teacher conferences that her teacher told me that Tom's parents are so thankful to Paris and how her friendship and interest in helping Tom had made their son's school experience the happiest it had ever been and that Tom looked forward to going to school . . . because Paris would be there. That brought me to tears. I too had a child with ADHD, an elder sibling of Paris's. I knew firsthand what it felt like to be the mother of an ADHD child who never fit in with the mainstream of anything. Watching my own ADHD child being excluded from activities and birthday parties because of "loud behavior" and having poor grades and few to no friends was at times excruciating. Yet here was a little girl in the fourth grade, my child, mentoring and loving her little Tom. Most assuredly, that was one of my proudest moments of being Paris's mother.

Being an excellent reader, Paris was voted by her peers to be the class "chapter reading" student. She would hold her audience for thirty minutes each morning for "Reading Corner." Her classmates loved reading time, and Paris, again, got to be "teacher," her most favorite thing to be and do.

It was around this time that Paris was hooked on the Harry Potter series. She had them all. I recall standing in a long line outside the bookstore with Paris and Helen at midnight. The girls wanted to be there for the first of the book sales. I smile as I recall Helen holding her new book up to my face when she said to me

"Smell the pages, Mummy!"

Now divorced and a single mother, I had to find ways of coming up with the money for books for my girls. They would easily read two books a week, and I did not begrudge the cost. There was a time, while at the cash register of a bookstore, the girls said it would be good if I could work there and get some free books. The cashier smiled and said it was 40 percent off for employees and that they were hiring. I started the next weekend while the girls spent time with their dad at his apartment. My whole paycheck, and then some, was spent on books, which did not work out at all because I was still overspending!

I was a college student myself at this time, and Paris took great interest in my Texas history textbook and was delighted when I agreed that she could be my quiz master and ask me the questions at the end of each chapter. She would soon let me know if I got an answer wrong.

"Did you read the chapter, Mummy?"

"Yes!"

"Well, I don't think you are paying attention, Mummy!"

"Excuse me, Miss Teacher, ma'am, that is not how you talk to your mother!"

"Sorry, I was just trying to help you!"

I would give her one of my looks that let her know she had said enough. Still she persisted,

"If you just read one page at a time and paid attention, you would get it. That's how I get my As, Mummy"

Okay, she was not giving up, and she did have a point. So I humbled myself and agreed that I would study just one page at a time and then she could give me the quiz from the end of the chapter.

Texas and American history were not my favorite subjects, and I had little interest in the quizzes, but they were mandatory for my degree. It was true that my grades were poor in these two subjects, and who was I to argue with someone who knows how to get As? Paris and Helen also insisted that I post my grades on the refrigerator door just like they had to do.

"I will be your teacher, Mummy, but you have to pay attention. Paying attention is very important"

"Paris, you are being a tad rude, you know."

At that, Paris ran into her bedroom and cried. I let her be for a bit to see if she could work it out for herself. Who was wrong here, Paris for being so forward to her mother or me for being prideful? I went in to see her, and I told her I was sorry and that I appreciated her wanting to help me but that I still expected her to . . . what? Was this my pride getting in the way here? Paris still insisted I needed to pay attention. Arguing wasn't worth it. Being my teacher was important to her, and since she was my fourth child, I had learned to pick my battles. She won!

Chapter 8

THE DAY THAT WOULD FOREVER CHANGE OUR LIVES

*I*t was an especially happy Sunday morning. We had already been to church, and on the way home, we drove to the new subdivision in South Austin, Texas. We had just recently received a phone call in the past week from the mortgage company to say that my mortgage loan application was approved and that we could go ahead and pick out our lot, the floor plan, and colors of carpet and tile that we wanted. We were so excited that evening that we went out for dinner.

We had driven the short three miles to the new subdivision to stand on the lot that the girls and I knew would be just perfect to build our new house, our happy home. We chose a lot facing southwest so that we could have a backyard on the northeast of the house to give us shade in the backyard on those hot and humid Texas summer afternoons.

Paris stood on the spot where she knew her new bedroom would be. Helen did the same. I was busy standing where my new kitchen would be, looking out to the large backyard area and feeling very happy knowing that my little girls would soon have a backyard to play in, and that it would be shaded from the hot afternoon sun.

The apartment we were living in was beautiful, but I knew it was temporary. We had rented out our family house to go to Japan, and the tenants loved living there and wanted to stay for another year. It was a big five-bedroom, four-bathroom house and way too big for just the three of us, so we took an apartment until our circumstances changed. The girls, now eight and nine years old, needed a safe place to run and play and a backyard to play in. At last our dream was about to come true; just four months to build and we would be so happy.

We got home, eventually, and changed into comfortable clothes and were looking forward to the pot roast with apple pie and ice cream to follow. This was a day to celebrate!

As a single mother and two young girls, this was a particularly happy time in our lives.

Paris and Helen were typical in their behavior of eight- and nine-year-olds, respectively. Despite being told not to run in the house, they did; it was then that Paris knocked a glass flying from the dinner table. Having been chastised for her behavior, Paris just started giggling and insisting, "I can't help knocking into things because I'm wobbly."

She was laughing so hard that tears were rolling down her face. I asked Paris what she meant when she said she was feeling wobbly.

"When I walk up straight, I wobble!"

Her laughter continued. Now Helen and I could not help but laughing with her.

"If I bend my head sideways, I don't wobble!"

More laughter continued.

My own laughter was quick to subside. I asked Paris to come to me and I lifted her pretty little face up to mine. I could see a difference in her eye movements.

"Do you have any pain? Do your ears hurt?"

"No."

Then she burst into laughter again as she said, "You look as if you have four eyes, Mummy!"

It was then I recalled an occasion a few days previous when I had noticed her written school homework looked like hen-scratchings. For her age, eight years and ten months, she usually had nice penmanship. I just had a sinking feeling in my stomach, and took her on my lap to give her a hug. All that was going through my head were her words:

"You have four eyes, Mummy!"

Recalling her poor handwriting, I cuddled her into me, and as I stroked her silky brown hair, it came to me to get her to the hospital.

"Why have you not told me you were seeing double, Paris?"

"Because I didn't want you to keep me out of school!"

I said nothing to my girls except to go get their shoes on and get their jackets. I went into my bedroom and called my family doctor. It was Sunday, and my call went to some other service, and all they could say was take her to her doctor in the morning, or if she was in pain to take her to the emergency room. Paris was not in any pain, but she was having a vision problem. When she walked across the living room with her head held to one side, her vision was good, but when she walked or held her head straight up her vision became doubled. I wasn't a doctor, but there is this thing called mother's intuition.

We got to the emergency room, and all I could tell the doctor was, "Paris is seeing double."

The doctor checked her out, and, lo and behold, everything checked out okay. She was walking straight, and her eyesight was perfect. However, when the doctor went to get the checkout paperwork together, Paris said, "Mummy, I can see two phones on the wall, and there was only one there a minute ago."

The doctor came back with the checkout papers. I told him.

"We won't be leaving right now, Paris is seeing double again."

The doctor looked at me with that look that says, "overanxious mother." He was very nice and smiled, saying, "Since Paris is not in any pain, you should start off by taking her to see her primary care physician in the morning."

I was insistent when I said, "I prefer that we take care of Paris here and now."

"Okay, we could take an X-ray."

"Okay, let's do it!"

Off Paris went, holding the doctor's hand, looking back at Helen, and laughing all the way as she and her sister already agreed that the young doctor looked cute. This did give the attitude of larking around, but I was sure there was something more going on, and I know that our primary care physician could not see inside Paris's head. The mother's intuition was still nagging at me.

Paris had been gone for her X-ray for what seemed like forever, but it was really only for a half hour or so. Then the doctor came back carrying Paris in his arms, and the two of them were laughing. Then the doctor looked at me and said, "Let's go into my office for a chat."

I had a tremendous sense of calm in me, but at the same time I knew I was going to be told bad news. The doctor, still carrying Paris now over his shoulder as a father would playfully do with his child, led the way.

I took Helen's hand, and I followed. Once inside the office, the doctor pulled out a chair for me to sit on, and he sat down opposite me, setting Paris on his lap. Our eyes met, and I could see the moistness in his eyes.

He said, "The X-ray shows that Paris has a mass deep in her head, but that is all I can say at this point. I have already made an appointment for Paris to see a neurosurgeon at 8:00 a.m. tomorrow morning."

Handing me the appointment card with a trembling hand, the doctor kept hold of Paris as if she were his own. I took the card and smiled at the doctor, knowing this was hard for him and that he may well know more than he is telling me but needs more than an X-ray to confirm the worst possible diagnosis. Cancer definitely crossed my mind, but I didn't want to believe that it could happen to my family.

It was evening and dark outside as we left the hospital. Helen and Paris were in the backseat of the car, laughing at whatever little girls find to giggle about. It would be Halloween in a few days, and that was all they could think about, both still undecided what they were going to dress up as. It had been raining while we were in the hospital and now was coming down like a monsoon; the roads were wet. I sat at a red light and watched the windscreen wipers swipe from side to side, almost as if they were wiping away tears. The doctor never did say the dreaded "C" word, but I knew deep in me that my baby girl had cancer.

The red light was in no hurry to change to green. I sat there holding the steering wheel in an eerie calmness. I had no tears. I looked at both of my young daughters in the rearview mirror. I could see them laughing, but I could no longer hear them. My world had become silent and still, and all I could think was that their lives would never be the same. At some point the light changed to green, but my thoughts were elsewhere until the loud sound of the horn honking repeatedly from the car behind prompted me back to reality. A different kind of reality.

Once home, we had dinner, though it had somehow lost its flavor, and, since it was now late, I got the girls ready for bed. We followed the same routine as usual, but how long would our family's routine stay normal? Tucked in their matching twin beds, Helen and Paris both looked the picture of health. I read the usual bedtime stories, but I didn't want the stories to end; the land of fairy tales was an escape, for now. The end of the stories meant lights out, then I would have to sit by myself and the thoughts of cancer would haunt me.

I called the number for the house in Louisiana, where my former husband was visiting and left a message for him to return my call, but he was already on his way back to Austin. I was a single mother and my eldest two children had already left the nest, both serving in the military. While I had many friends I could have called, I didn't. I wanted to wait to see what the surgeon had to say in the morning. Or maybe I just didn't want to make the situation more real by talking about it. I then recalled my pregnancy with Paris, the scare of spina bifida and Down syndrome that never was and the needless hell I put myself through. Was I just doing the same thing to myself all over again?

I sat outside in the cool air. It never really got too cold in Texas in late October. Not like my own country of Scotland, where the weather could get bitter cold at this time of year. The coolness felt good; I thought it would help me think clearly. But it was as if I was in some sort of dream. What was there to think about? Did I really take my child to the emergency room today? Do we really have a brain surgeon's appointment in the morning? What had just happened today? I was drawing a blank. Numb.

I got up and went into the girls' bedroom. I sat on the edge of Paris's bed and looked at her. I could see her petite features in the moonbeam coming through the window. She looked peaceful as she slept, and I caressed her little head and felt the silkiness of her hair. Looking across at Helen, I saw she too was fast asleep, her beautiful long blonde hair with soft curls cascading across her pillow and down the side of the bed. Amazing the girls had the same parents, but the only feature they had in common was their noses. I looked around their bedroom and saw the many cuddly toys that the girls had acquired over the years. They did share many of their toys with each other, but not their books. Each girl had to have her own books. They were both avid readers for their ages, and both had their own bookcases full of books, with Harry Potter being the favorite.

I wandered into my bathroom to take care of my own bedtime routine, but I just stood there looking into the mirror. I quickly gave myself a little pat on the check and told myself to snap out of it, to wake up. The doctor did not say cancer; he said a mass, a shadow. Try as I might, I could not snap out of it. I wandered around my bedroom looking at the little treasures on my dresser that my children had given me over the years, recalling the occasions in which they were given, many of which brought smiles to my face.

I didn't quite know what to do next. What was I supposed to be doing? Weren't we just running and jumping around on our new lot just a few hours ago? Weren't we just standing in our soon-to-be-built house, imagining the backyard that will be played in? What had happened since this morning? This was a 180-degree turnaround!

I sat down on the couch, and the clock on the mantle over the fireplace came to life as it struck out its beautiful Westminster chime. It was 11:00 p.m. The next thing I was aware of was the clock striking 5:00 a.m. Where had those hours in between gone? I was still sitting up straight on the couch. Had I slept? Was all this just a bad dream, a mother's nightmare? Please let me wake up. Again my thoughts retuned to my pregnancy. God answered my prayers then, and he would come through for me again this time too. Stupid me, where was my faith?

Helen and Paris, Austin, Texas, 1998

Chapter 9

THE 8:00 A.M. SURGEON'S APPOINTMENT

The commute to the surgeon's office took longer than I had anticipated; I felt myself gripping the steering wheel with white knuckles. The truth was that I was scared; I didn't want to be going to this appointment. I had dropped Helen off at school, and Paris had a million questions about why she couldn't go see the doctor after school. Paris loved school, and her voice seemed to be fading in and out while I drove. I had left home early enough to allow for the heavy traffic; every traffic light was red. It was as if my car was on autopilot, as if it knew where it was going. It was as if my brain was going numb. My mind was drifting between the past and the present. I was trying to convince myself that this was much ado about nothing. A mass could be caused by several things . . . but what? What else could it be?

The waiting room was empty. The woman behind the desk was very pleasant for such an early hour. I filled out the obligatory paperwork, pages of it, but I could not remember the answers to simple questions, and it was painstaking. I had a hard time remembering some of the most basic information.

A nurse was quick to appear, and she walked us through to the triage area. The surgeon had already received Paris's X-rays by courier. All her vital numbers were that of a healthy child. I watched her as she was standing on the scale. Her hair was reflecting the bright lights from the ceiling. Paris loved her hair—it was a medium brown, very straight, cut in a bob, and naturally very glossy, unlike Helen's, whose hair was a dark blonde with natural long ringlets. I found myself smiling, thinking I was wrong about this mass in her head; after all, she looked the picture of a healthy little girl.

The surgeon soon appeared and looked like Santa Claus in a white coat. He was jovial and smiling. My heart was racing at the anticipation of this mass being something, anything, other than cancer. Why else would the surgeon be talking to Paris so lightheartedly? He wanted to know what book she had brought to read. Paris was quick to tell him, "It's Harry Potter of course!"

This big Santa Claus of a man sat and listened to Paris's overview of Harry Potter for at least ten minutes. The whole conversation had nothing to do with why we were all there in his office at eight o'clock on a Monday morning.

The surgeon scribbled a note on a small pad of paper, then told Paris, "I want you to come back and see me again, Paris, and tell me some more about Harry Potter."

He opened the office door and called for the nurse in the hallway; she came in and then escorted Paris out. After Paris had walked out the door, the surgeon closed the door, leaving me alone in the office with him. He handed me the note he had written, his face without mirth. Santa Claus had disappeared and was replaced by a look of blankness, neither happy nor sad. He said, "I looked at Paris's X-rays this morning. She cannot have anything to eat or drink after 6:00 p.m. Bring her to the Children's Hospital at Brackenridge at 5:00 a.m. tomorrow morning. We are going to have a look inside and see what is causing the mass."

So the nightmare continued. Well, what else should I have expected? Of course he was going to act lighthearted in the presence of a child patient. But his change in demeanor just seemed to underscore my worst fears. Still, no one had yet said the "C" word, only me, and only in my mind.

Paris was impatient to get to school and not too concerned about the appointment. Children seem to be able to let things go much more easily than adults, who hold on to the unknown and make it out to be as bleak as possible. Or maybe that's just a mom thing, always thinking the worst when it comes to their kids. All my worry during my pregnancy with Paris turned out to be needless—could I be making the same mistake?

Paris ran to her class and I went into the school office. I had already decided that I was not going to say more than I had to. I just told the office the Paris would not be at school tomorrow, that she needed surgery, and that she may be out of school for two weeks. What else could I say?

I drove home in a blur. What was happening to me, to Paris, to our little family that was so happy just forty-eight hours earlier?

I called Paris's father and told him about the appointment, and he agreed to meet us there the next morning. I guess I went through the motions for most of the day. I was a student myself, but classes and homework were the farthest things from my mind. I did manage to get together some items for Paris's hospital stay and some essentials for myself. The thought that my little girl was going to have brain surgery in the morning scared me, yet I knew it was going to take place whether I was worried or not, scared or not. I made arrangements with my good friend Sue, who would take care of Helen after she came home from school. In the meantime, I kept my fears to myself.

I was exhausted, yet I had done nothing physical. My mind was relentless, my thoughts never ending, like a car engine just revving and revving but going nowhere. I don't know how many times I paced around the apartment, aimlessly picking things up just to lay them down again. I prepared the meat sauce for spaghetti bolognaise, the girls' favorite, and planned to have the ice cream left over from Sunday. Paris would have nothing else after her meal.

I picked the girls up from school as usual; that was the only normal thing I had done all day. My girls never took the school bus. I drove them to school every morning, and then I would drive the few short miles to campus to work on my own degree. The Texas history that I was studying was my least favorite class; however, Paris enjoyed what I had to learn, elected to be my mentor, or teacher, as she called herself, and kept me going when the going got rough.

Seeing their two smiling faces as they ran toward my car gave me my first reason to smile for the day. How I loved them both! These two little girls were the babies I never thought I would have; how blessed I had been. I and my two older children were Scots, but both Helen and Paris were born in Albuquerque, New Mexico, after we emigrated in 1989.

It felt so good to have them home. Why had I taken that so much for granted? They made a beeline for a snack of fruit and juice after every school day. Homework was next on the agenda. Dinner was served, and both girls were delighted to have ice cream too. I just listened to them chatter away at the dinner table as young girls do; typically it would be about what cute boy was new in their classes. Strangely, Paris never mentioned her appointment from that morning. I never mentioned it either, somehow trying to put it off and out of my mind.

I never told Paris that she could not eat or drink anything else for the evening. I knew if I did it would naturally just make her want what she could not have. Instead, I just kept an eye on the girls and the refrigerator door. Neither of the girls wanted to eat or drink for the rest of the evening. Our late-evening routine went as it always did: bath, brush teeth, pj's, stories, prayers, and then lights out.

This night was to be a repeat of the night before. I set the alarm clock to make sure I would not oversleep, but I did not sleep at all. I got myself into the shower. I thought that the running water would help make me feel better, or wake me up, but it didn't. I was confused, I was afraid, I was tired, I was a mess. I walked around the apartment looking at this and that, but nothing was registering. I was on autopilot in the kitchen cleaning up, almost like a robot. The dark of night was giving way to the dawn, and yet another day was before me.

What was in store for Paris today and what was in store for the life I once knew? I was feeling a little strange, a part of me was very sleepy, yet I was awake, but having a nightmare all at the same time. I could not make sense of anything.

Paris, age 3½, Austin, Texas

Chapter 10

THE DAY OF SURGERY

I was sitting at the kitchen table looking at the builder's blue print and floor plan of what was to be our new house, a home for the three of us. Then the alarm clock in my bedroom rang. The sound of its loud bell was as if it was announcing a day of doom.

I got the girls up and dressed. I had Sue pick up Helen almost immediately, so Helen would have breakfast at Sue's home so as not to tempt Paris with food. Paris was protesting that she needed breakfast before she went to school. I had not told Paris that she was to have brain surgery this morning, or that she will be out of school for at least a couple of weeks. Why tell her; let her have her peace of mind for now. I was worried enough for both of us.

"Paris, honey, you won't be having anything to eat right now until we see the doctor again this morning."

As gently as I could, I told her, "The doctor that you told all about Harry Potter wants, well, he wants to help you see better, and we are going to see him again this morning."

Paris protested, "I need to go to school, Mummy. Can't we go to the doctor's after school?"

I just held her and said, "We need to get your eyes good again so you can do your schoolwork."

Paris was a good kid and rarely complained about anything, but having to miss school was not going over too well. Now there were tears.

She cried, "It's not fair. I was working on my craft project today, and I was going to do reading corner too."

The hospital was in downtown Austin, and the traffic was getting heavy. This was not a good morning so far, and I knew it was only going to get worse. I parked the car in the parking garage of the hospital and was about to get Paris's bag and my own out of the trunk, then I thought, *No, I don't need her to see the bags yet*, and left them there. As we walked along the pathway to the entrance, I couldn't help but notice all the traffic speeding along the highway, thinking of all those drivers possibly going to work and only worrying about what deadline they had to meet. I wondered if any of those drivers saw a woman walking with her little girl into the hospital and what their day was like. Probably not.

I held on to Paris's hand tightly. So many thoughts and questions were going through my head: What would this day bring, how would it end, and why was this happening? Yet a part of me was saying it was all a repeat of my worrying when I was pregnant and that God heard my prayers then, and he would hear them this time too. I needed to have faith and not worry.

We were met by a wonderful team of pediatric nurses. They all put Paris at ease quickly. I, however, was hanging on to my fear like it was something to cherish. The word *surgery* was never spoken in Paris's presence. The first order of the day was the triage, and all was good. Next was the MRI. The surgeon showed me the films, but frankly I did not know what I was looking at.

Before too long, Paris was given a sedative and was soon asleep. She was put on a gurney, and I walked alongside it holding her little hand. I walked with her as far as I was allowed to, then I had to let go. A nurse walked with me to the intensive care unit waiting room and told me the surgery would be about three hours and that there was a phone in the waiting room, where I was to receive updates from the operating room, and that I would get a call soon. After twenty minutes, I got the first call to say that Paris was under anesthesia and that the surgery was underway.

Sitting in the ICU waiting room was somewhat of an awakening for me. Other families were there too, waiting for news of their loved one. The phone in the waiting room rang frequently, and, each time it did, everyone stood up, and then someone would pick it up, hoping it was good news. I then positioned myself next to the phone and elected myself as the phone operator for the waiting room; time and again the calls were for everyone but me, and I wasn't too anxious for my call as the nurse did say the surgery would be about three hours.

After an hour and a half, the phone rang yet again. By then I had gotten used to standing up as I answered, ready to call out the family name, but this time it was for "the mother of Paris Acree." I held the phone with a vise-like grip and slowly sat down again.

"Paris will be coming out shortly. Her surgery is over," said the nurse from the operating room. I put the phone down on its cradle slowly. I could feel every eye in the waiting room on me. One woman came up to me and put her arm around me and asked, "Is your little girl going to be okay?"

"I don't know. It has only been an hour and a half, and they said it would be three! I don't know what to think."

I took my place outside the waiting room, keeping my eyes peeled on the door to the surgery, where they took Paris less than two hours before. I don't know how long I stood there; I felt as if I were in a dream. The fact that the surgery took much less time than expected made me uneasy. *But what if that's good news! Maybe it was an abscess or something and all will be well. Yes,* I thought, *God did hear my prayers again. What other reason could there be? How stupid of me, worrying myself sick over something like an abscess; why do I always think the worst when it comes to my kids! All the girls and I need to be thinking about right now are the colors we want for our new house!*

I was so lost in my thoughts that I did not see the big doors swing open. Before I knew it, the gurney passing by me held my little Paris. I almost lost my breath as I looked at her head swathed in bandages. I could barely see the small features of her face. The surgeon put his hand on my shoulder and told me the nurse would take Paris to the recovery room. He looked at me and paused.

"Paris has an astrocytoma. She has brain cancer, and the tumor is growing out of her brain stem. I cut it back as far as I could, which will give her temporary relief of her vision problem, but she has a long way to go."

Despite all of my worrying, I was shocked at the news. I could feel my gut twisting in a knot at the confirmation. I headed straight to the ladies room and threw up. I washed up and looked at myself in the mirror.

"My baby girl has brain cancer!" I said out loud to the face in the mirror, the reflection of me that had aged dramatically within a couple of days, with sunken eyes and black circles under them. I just stood there looking into the mirror. I knew I was standing there, but I felt that a part of me was far off somewhere else, a weird feeling racing through me. I threw up some more. *God, where are you?*

I went to the recovery room to see Paris, and there were two nurses attending her. Paris was waking up slowly and, when she saw me, she gave a weak smile. I gave her a kiss, and she closed her eyes again. The nurses said that she would sleep for a while. The nurse asked me to go with her to the surgeon's area to talk with him.

"Paris will recover well from today's surgery, her vision will be greatly improved. In fact, I expect it to be back to normal functioning for a while anyway. However, this will be temporary because the tumor will continue to grow. I will have the nurse set up appointments for radiation and chemotherapy right away, and all her treatment can be taken care of locally."

I really thought I was having a bad dream—a nightmare—and at any moment I was going to wake up. This is not what the outcome was supposed to be. I took the paperwork from the nurse and walked into the hallway. The nurse said that Paris would be moved to her own room in about an hour and to come back at that time. It was hard to breathe. I had what felt like a large lump in my throat and a tightness in my chest; I walked outside for some air. It was as if there was no air to breathe, and my legs felt like jelly. Luckily there was a bench just outside the door, and I sat down and threw up again. While the bile was burning my throat, I just sat there as if in a stupor. I didn't know what was happening to me; I didn't know which end was up, where I was, or what I was doing. *Don't I just have to pick out the carpet and the colors for the new house?*

After a while, I collected what sanity I had left, and my Scottish blood started pumping. I went to Paris's room and there she was, asleep and wearing her turban of bandages. I just sat and held her hand for a while until I felt it move. She opened her eyes and smiled.

"Will I be going back to school today, Mummy?"

"No, sweetheart, not today."

She tried to sit up, and her small hand reached for her head.

"What happened, Mummy?"

"You had a surgery, sweetheart. Your eyesight should be better now."

"Oh, yes, you only have two eyes now."

As she laughed, it caused her head to hurt; she lifted her hand to her head and felt the bandages.

"What is all this on my head?"

Paris was a smart little cookie, and she had many questions. I knew better than to belittle her condition to her anymore. I told her of the mass in her head, and she took it all matter-of-factly. I thought of her tender years that she did not know just how bad her diagnosis was, and I did not feel the need to elaborate any further.

The nurse was kind and attentive; she sat down and told Paris about her own children and that she felt lucky to be the one to take care of her for the next few days. Paris was very alert for having just gone through brain surgery a few hours earlier. But then she lay back on her pillow and fell asleep. Her nurse said that she was doing great and that I might want to go home and get some sleep too, but I was wide awake and told the nurse that I would be spending the night at Paris's bedside. I just wanted to be close to her, maybe more for myself than her. I needed her that night.

I called Sue's house to check up on Helen; I wanted to hear my daughter's sweet little voice. She was having fun and getting ready for bed; it was a sleepover for her, and she was happy. Sue would take her to school the next morning with her own children.

I walked out to my car and collected the bags that I had packed, thinking how my world had changed since I had packed them the night before. The night air was cool on my face, which felt hot and swollen. An *astrocytoma*, the doctor had said. Just a fancy word for brain cancer. Why does the word *cancer* have such a scary and "final" sound to it?

The nurse brought me a reclining chair and a blanket. She was so nice, later bringing me some hot chocolate. I found it hard to sit still; I paced around Paris's room like a lioness protecting her cub, the only difference being that I did not protect my little cub, I did not stop the cancer, and neither did God. *Why?* I was still asking myself if this was all really happening.

I started all the crazy self-talk, like *What has my child done to deserve this? What have I done to deserve this?* I knew a little child did not deserve this, and, while I had my imperfections, no way did I deserve this either. *Okay, at any moment I will wake up. This is surely a nightmare. It's not real, and it's not really happening.* But there was Paris swathed in bandages. *It's real, and it is happening, so get over it, Vikki, and do what you need to do.*

Before I knew it, it was morning. Paris woke up and said her head hurt, so I got the nurse in right away, and she was given some mild pain relief. She even managed to eat a full breakfast while I looked on in amazement. Things were not adding up for me. Apart from the bandages, this kid seemed quite normal.

"When will I be able to go back to school, Mummy?"

"I don't know, Paris, just as soon as the doctor says you can."

The words were no sooner out of my mouth when Sue and two of Paris's teachers showed up to visit, and they had brought Helen with them. Paris was elated. Goodness, there were so many flowers and stuffed animals and cards from the school. Paris sat up and read every card and was almost buried under all her new teddies; multicolored balloons filled the room; the surroundings looked more like a carnival than a hospital room.

After Sue and her teachers had spent most of the day visiting, they left and Helen stayed. Paris was feeling tired and just wanted to sleep. The nurse said that Paris was recovering well from the surgery and her sleepiness was normal. I decided to go home that night to shower and wash away the odor that had built up over two days. I was also aware that Helen needed some one-on-one Mummy-time too. Paris said that she wanted her own pajamas and her Harry Potter book. I took her orders, of which there would be many to follow, and we drove home. Helen took it badly that Paris would be in hospital for a few days, and she cried. I decided to keep her close to me, and when we got home, I let her pick out pajamas for Paris and get her Harry Potter book.

Helen was a more sensitive child than her siblings, and her young heart was easily broken. I didn't just have Paris to worry about, but the whole family and how they would take the news. I kept Helen out of school the next day and took her to the hospital with me. The little sisters were happy to see each other and Paris's bandage turban was the topic of laughter. I could not believe what light they made of it, just laughing and joking as if it were only a headdress, while all the while it was covering a monster growing inside Paris's brain stem. The laughter gave way to pain for Paris, and the nurse suggested that she have a mild sedative and to put her turbaned head back on her pillow and get a good nights' sleep. We all agreed. I had originally wanted to spend the night at the hospital, but I knew that I had my work cut out for me finding the best surgeon and hospital in the world for my girl. I couldn't accept that a local cancer center would do; I wanted the best for her. So there were endless hugs and kisses, and we stayed long enough to watch Paris fall asleep, then Helen and I drove home.

It had been a long day for us both, and although Helen was very tired, she had endless questions about Paris. The girls were both very close and were best friends as well as sisters. I gave minimal answers that seemed to satisfy her questions, and she had been happy to see that Paris was laughing and joking. I knelt beside Helen at her bedside as she prayed. Normally Helen, in her shyness, said her prayers silently to herself, but this evening she needed no encouragement to pray out loud. I wept as I listened to this little girl plead to God to allow her little sister to get better and come home; on and on she prayed, and it was obvious that she was afraid. I felt so helpless! Here were two little girls, my girls, one terminally ill, and the other afraid and scared, and here I am, their mother, but I could do nothing to ease their pain. Tucked in bed reading her own Harry Potter book, Helen soon fell asleep.

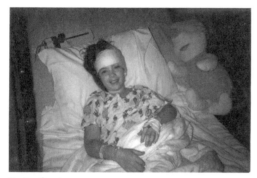

Paris after her surgery

Chapter 11

THE LONG NIGHT BEGINS

The phone rang many times that night, but I didn't want to answer it. The caller ID told me it was not the hospital. The callers were friends with questions. I didn't want to give more information than I had to; that would mean acknowledging the truth, and I wasn't ready for that. I needed to think. What has happened? This is something that you hear about on the local news or at the corner shop about some other family on the other end of town. Not my family! Not my child! This was foreign territory to me. Where would I even start? I called the hospital to make sure Paris was still okay, and the nurse on the phone had assured me that they would call me if she woke up.

I turned on my computer and started looking up as many cancer treatment centers as I could find, including hospitals in London, England; Paris, France; and Victoria, Australia. I read through the night about child brain cancer, only to find that I was not the only mother with a broken heart. There were so many websites on childhood brain cancer, so tragic.

I did all the laundry, got it dried and ironed, and piled it up on my dresser. I looked for the passports for Paris and me and left a voice mail for my real estate agent to put my former home, now a rental property, on the market. I was getting ready to go wherever I needed to go no matter the cost. I was desperate and willing to mortgage my very soul to find a cure for Paris.

The morning soon came, and, with no sleep, I drove to the hospital to see Paris. I spent all day with her, and she was smiling and laughing. By the evening I was starting to feel drunk from the lack of sleep. Paris suggested I go home, that she was okay. I felt miserable, and the darkness of the night made me feel alone. Home again, I was back at the computer and drinking mugs full of coffee to keep me awake as I continued searching for the best possible cancer doctors and treatments I could find for my girl.

There was one specialist's name that came up over and over again, Park. His name was mentioned internationally. I had to find this guy. Before I knew it, Helen was standing by my side.

"Can't you sleep, sweetheart?"

"It's time to get up for school, Mummy!"

I don't know where all the hours went. I lost all track of time. I was wide awake and didn't feel tired at all but nervous and jumpy. While Helen had cereal and toast for breakfast that day, I wasn't hungry. Things with her seemed to be okay on the surface; she was a little more clingy than usual and often preferred to sleep in my bed, but I think she may have been suppressing a lot of her feelings. It would be her tenth birthday in a few days, and she was looking forward to being in double digits. My girls were never demanding kids, and Helen would be happy with books as gifts.

I had been at the computer all night long. I was past being tired, and I was feeling light-headed. My search for Mr. Park lead me through endless phone calls where I would be passed around among ten different people and invariably be put on hold.

I drove Helen to school and then drove to our primary care physician's office. Dr. Poon had taken care of our family since we had moved to Texas four years earlier. She was expecting me, as she had received updates from the hospital. She was not only an amazing doctor, but she was also the mother of two young girls. I talked to her about the elusive Mr. Park. She assisted in the research and found out that he was in New York.

While visiting Paris in the hospital later that day, our doctor's office called to say that Mr. Park would be visiting St. Jude Children's Research Hospital in Memphis, Tennessee. Dr. Poon called on my behalf, and St. Jude asked for a sample of Paris's cancer cells and MRI films from her recent surgery in Austin. The Children's Hospital at Brackenridge gave me the special package, and I took it to the nearest FedEx office and had it sent overnight priority. The rest of the day was hard to get through. I was sure if anyone could save my little girl's life, it would be Mr. Park.

Paris was feeling so amazingly well, and had all good numbers, so by the end of the day her doctor said she could go home in the morning. This was great news. For some reason I wanted desperately to be at home with my two girls and lock the door. I was feeling afraid, insecure, and vulnerable. I felt my whole world was being ripped away from me and that I had no control over anything. This cancer monster was running the show and dictating my life and that of my girls. It was an eerie feeling.

I went home that night and picked Helen up from Sue's house. Helen was so happy to know that her sister would be home in the morning. Little did she know that this was just the beginning, I never did tell her that Paris was not cured of the cancer or that she was terminally ill and not out of the woods yet. I guess I just did not want to break her young heart any sooner than I had to. It was her birthday soon, and all appeared to be well in her little world . . . for today anyway.

The next morning after another night of pacing the floor, I kept Helen home from school, and we picked Paris up from the hospital and drove straight home and locked the door as if our apartment held the crown jewels; my girls were my crown jewels, and I wanted them safe. But my mind was plagued with the thought that we brought the cancer home with us.

The girls wanted a pizza party that evening, and I agreed. I called for a pizza delivery, and we broke all the rules about not eating in the living room. We then cuddled up in my big bed, and Paris and Helen took turns at reading Happy Potter out loud. It was a happy evening, and the girls and I feel asleep. I think it was the first sleep I'd had in several days.

I was awakened and startled by the phone around 7:30 p.m. The caller ID said it was a Tennessee number. It was a call from Jenn at St. Jude. She said that they wanted to invite Paris to participate in a new protocol. I was overjoyed—at last my baby would be in the top facility with the top doctors, and for sure her life would be saved. I quickly made phone calls for Helen to be taken care of in my absence. It would be her birthday in two days and the first birthday that I would have to miss. I left the girls to sleep in my bed, and I grabbed suitcases and packed a bag for Helen and one for Paris and myself. The plane tickets had been reserved for us, and all I had to do was just wait for morning. Again I spent the remainder of the night pacing around. Sometimes I would pinch myself to see if I was awake, or at least to wake myself up. I really, honestly felt that I was having a bad dream, and that I would wake up at any minute.

Chapter 12

DASH TO THE AIRPORT

Sue came at 6:00 a.m. to take Helen. It was Helen's birthday the next day, and I wasn't sure how long I would be gone, so it was hard to say good-bye. But while it was not easy to leave her behind, taking her with me would surely have been a miserable experience for her. Sue was so kind to say she would have a birthday cake for her and a little birthday party.

The taxi was supposed to pick us up at 6:30 a.m. The pick-up time came and went. Now anxiety was like a great weight on my chest. The cab finally showed up at 6:45 a.m., just fifteen minutes late, but that fifteen minutes was the start of a day that was going straight downhill. Yes, I let the cab driver know that I was less than happy at his lateness, and I was none too polite about it either; in fact, I was rather horrible. The driver apologized and assured me that he would have me at the airport in plenty of time for our fight. He asked about our airline and destination. I was angry, though, at what, I didn't know. Actually, I did know. It was the cancer. I was feeling cheated. I took good care of my kids, always made sure they took my hand crossing the street, made sure they were always safe and protected, took them for their well-child checkups every year, took them to the dentist every six months, and would absolutely put myself between them and any danger. But now there was this demon from hell that was in Paris's head and I could not do a thing about it. I was angry—big time!

On telling the cab driver that we were flying to Florida, he asked, "Oh, are you going to Disney World?"

I was getting more annoyed by the minute. The anger was building in me.

"No, I'm taking my little girl to St. Jude's. We are connecting to a Memphis flight from Florida."

I spat my words at him, in some way hoping that by doing so I would relieve myself of the pain I was feeling inside, but that didn't work; the pain became welded to my heart. All I had done was make this poor cab driver uncomfortable. Once at the airport, the driver was quick to get out and assist with our bags. He looked me in the eye and said he was sorry. He would not take the cash from my hand for the fare. After he drove away, I felt absolutely ashamed for the way I had treated him. He didn't deserve my anger and tirade; he was just in the wrong place at the wrong time, and I was taking no hostages.

Paris was excited to be going on the plane; she enjoyed flying, more so when she had a seat at the window. She loved to point out as many things as possible and was disappointed when the cloud cover blocked her view of the land. I sat there, feeling more at ease now that we were buckled in our seats. The journey was now on its way—in more ways than one.

Overhearing many of the passengers' conversations, it would seem that many *were* going to Disney World. There was much laughter from children, and the child in front of me was peeking at me between the seats. Usually, I would have responded with a smile, but today I was not in a smiley mood, thinking, *These kids are going to Disney World, and my little Paris is going to St. Jude's. How freaking unfair is that?* My insides were becoming volcanic. I was recalling my pregnancy with her, the fear of spina bifida, then Down syndrome. *I guess God was just spinning me and Paris along, waiting to throw the big one at us. What have we done to deserve this?* Paris was busy looking out the window, and I just sat there looking at her. The turban bandage was already off as her incision was healing naturally and was covered over by her shiny brown hair.

My head talk had started again, almost like ten people all talking at once. They went on about how unfair it all was but must have exhausted themselves because soon all was quiet and still except for a few lingering questions. *Am I awake, or am I asleep and this is my nightmare? Am I sane or am I going mad?* Somewhere inside, I was tired, but I couldn't locate that place within me—I just kept doing what needed to be done.

It was time to fasten our seat belts again for landing. The flight was coming in on time and we had plenty of time to get to our connecting flight. Paris was cheerful, and it was her happy mood and healthy appearance that had my head so mixed up. She looked like a healthy kid! I was to repeat these words many times over the next few months.

Then Paris dropped her first of many bombshells on me.

"St. Jude's is a kid's hospital for kids dying of cancer, Mummy, isn't it?"

She had caught me off-guard. To this point I had never said anything to Paris about her diagnosis of cancer. I had only been talking to her about her eyesight and making sure she would not see double again. Where did she get the word *cancer* from? But I wasn't going to insult her by lying to her.

"Paris, St. Jude's is where children go to get cured of cancer. You don't need to be thinking like that. You're not going to die. We will find a cure!"

This was to be the start of many conversations with her. I should have planned telling her in a setting other than an airport lounge.

"I am," Paris said in a fit of giggles.

"You are what, baby?"

"I'm going to die!"

Paris was laughing out loud and thought it all so funny. I was taken aback.

The flight to Memphis dragged for the first half of the flight. I was anxious to get there and get the treatment to cure Paris. *Then in a few weeks—okay, a few months—this will all be behind us.* After all, her sight was back to normal.

Before I knew it, the plane was landing, and suddenly I wanted everything to slow down. I wasn't sure what was in store, but I wasn't ready for it.

A nice older gentleman was waiting at the baggage claim with a large, fun-looking sign, which read "Princess Paris Pardue Acree," and it was decorated in Disney characters. We walked up to the man and Paris said, "That's me!"

She had the biggest smile. He took our bags and walked us to a car in the waiting lane. I reminded the drama queen voice in my head to be on her good behavior. No angry words for the rest of the day.

St. Jude Children's Research Hospital

49

Chapter 13

DAY ONE AT ST. JUDE CHILDREN'S MEDICAL RESEARCH HOSPITAL

The private car pulled up at the archway at St. Jude Medical Research Hospital. I was happy to be there. For me it represented the cure that would be handed out by Mr. Park. At the same time, though, I was nervous, not knowing exactly what was going to happen next. Paris was taking it all in stride. Once inside the hallway, a staff member told us to stand in line at a check-in window. I thought that was strange, but stranger still was the sight of so many little children all in the same line. There was every skin tone and foreign language. Asian, Middle-Eastern, and I heard French and German. It was then that it hit me that cancer was ravaging the lives of so many children all over the world. I had been so ignorant of cancer and the illnesses of children because our family had been blessed with good health, to this point anyway. I was totally blown away at the sight of so many little children running up and down the hallways with their little bald heads, many with dark circles around their eyes—yet they laughed out loud. It was amazing.

Paris got her wristband with her personal information on it; this made her feel special in some odd way. It made me sick to my stomach. There was Paris taking it all in stride, and I was the proverbial basket case, thinking my kid's cancer was more important than the cancer of all the other kids. What was wrong with me? *For goodness' sake, Vikki, wake up to what is going on!* one of the many voices in my head was shouting.

The nurses at St. Jude must surely be angels dressed in scrubs: so kind, so loving, so caring. How do they cope with so many desperately ill children? Day after day they deal with these little ones—many bald and without eyebrows or eyelashes, their little eyes encircled with black shadows—yet these nurses are always smiling and cheering the kids on. Absolute angels.

Paris went through another triage, and all the numbers were good. Next was her physical examination, and all was good. I was having a hard time reconciling all of these good results with the fact that there was still cancer in her brain stem. Next we met several different doctors, all wonderful, loving men. None of them wore white coats, just jeans and shirts, looking like any child's dad or grandpa. They all spoke to Paris as if they were old buddies, so relaxed and easygoing.

Paris was taken for another MRI, and I got to go with her into the adjoining room with a large glass window. The size and look of that machine was mind-boggling. Paris's head was placed in the large dough-nut-like hole and the imaging began; the noise was that of knocking and whirling. It took a little time, but Paris managed to be perfectly still.

The images of the MRI were to be read by several doctors and neuro-surgeons, and I was shown to a small room to wait. I was wringing my hands and doing my usual pacing routine. I was pleased to know that many professionals would see Paris's films. *The more the better,* I thought. *All those great minds coming together to save my baby. Yes, this is going to be good. There will be a way, and all these doctors will be the ones to find that way, and, with my faith in God, this too shall pass.* I felt a little hope for the first time.

The door opened, and in came a nurse and a doctor. Dr. Steve, a New Yorker and the nicest guy you'd ever care to meet.

He looked at me, and I looked at him. He invited me to sit down. I always get a sinking feeling when I'm asked to sit down. He asked how I was holding up; he seemed to really care. He had a warmth about him that you don't always see in a doctor.

"We have a large team here and will do the best we can for Paris. We have done the MRI and considered it very carefully. First, the surgery that she had done in Texas was phenomenal. The tumor was cut back as far as it possibly could have been. The center of the tumor is inside the brain stem, which cannot be reached. The brain stem regulates Paris's breathing."

He asked me if I understood what he was saying, and I did. I told him just to please tell me as it is, to not hold anything back from me. I wanted the truth and to not give me false hope.

"Without doing anything else, Paris will have about three months to live. If we do chemotherapy first, she may have six months. If we do radiation first, followed possibly by chemotherapy she will have about nine months."

I sat there looking at him; he drew small pictures on the paper in front of me, showing where the brain stem was and how they would direct the radiation beam to her brainstem without touching other parts of her brain. Then I was waiting for the next option after the nine-month plan.

"Then . . . what comes after that?" I asked, waiting on the one treatment plan that would save her.

The doctor reached across the table and took my hand and said, "I'm so sorry, but short of a miracle, I can give Paris no more than nine months to live. You see, to go into her brain stem would be certain death. Nor can we radiate inside the brain stem, as that's what gives the lungs the signal to breathe. All we can do is give Paris a little more time. That is all we can do for this type of cancer: buy Paris a more little time."

I sat there, and the doctor's voice seemed to fade into the distance. He asked me if I understood what he was saying to me. I just nodded. He asked who I came with, and I told him no one, that I brought Paris by myself. He asked if he could call someone for me, and I said no. He sat with me for a while and asked about my family and things I generally like to do. He was just making conversation. What else could he say? The man just told a mother that her little girl was going to die.

Paris had had a very long day since we left Austin that morning. She had pretty much been turned upside down and inside out with this test and that test and was quite exhausted. She was peacefully sleeping and spent the night there, and I walked across the street to our hotel room.

As I got closer to the hotel, I just kept on walking, aimlessly. It was raining, but if I had noticed it at the time, I didn't care. I walked and walked. I felt so odd. I stopped and stood there on the sidewalk, noticing a bar with its glitzy lights flashing. In I went and sat on a tall barstool. The barmaid was all smiles and asked if I wanted to order something to eat or what would I like to drink. I just sat there and said nothing. I didn't know what I wanted. The woman asked me again if I wanted a drink, and I said yes.

"Give me a vodka and orange."

It had been many years since I'd had any alcohol; I thought with enough orange juice it would mask the horrible bitterness of the vodka.

The woman behind the bar was very pleasant and complimented me on my accent. That happens a lot.

"You're not from around here, are you?"

"No, I'm just visiting."

She poured the drink, and I gave it a sip; it was like poison! But I guess I looked stupid enough already, so I downed it! *Oh my gosh, do people actually like this stuff?* I didn't care. I thought I would just be a lady and be polite and just drink it. Then I asked for another double. She poured the poison again and I got it down better the second time. Then my head started to swoon, and I thought *I'm drunk, but who the hell cares?* I don't know how much I drank, but I guess I was starting to look foolish when the woman behind the bar asked me if I was all right. I paid the tab and left.

I had no idea where I was going or where I was for that matter. I stood against a wall and tried to remember. Ah, yes, the hotel. I started walking back the way I came and could see the top of the tall hotel in the distance. My high-heels were filled with water from the puddles, so I took them off. I decided to take a shortcut as the rain was pouring down by this time. I just kept my eyes on the top of the hotel. I heard a voice shouting, "Hey lady, you got a couple of dollars?"

I looked around and saw three young guys, and I was the only woman in sight, so I guess they were talking to me.

"Yeah, sure! How much do you want? You can have all the money I have."

After rummaging in my purse, I handed them my wallet. The guys were looking at me as if I were nuts, which I was. I told them if they had a gun, then to please go ahead and shoot me, as they would be doing me a favor. I told them in my best Scottish slur that my baby was up at St. Jude and they can only give her nine months to live. I was pathetic, but I didn't care. The three young guys said they were sorry and that I should just get to my hotel. They didn't take any money from me.

I staggered toward the hotel and sat under a large tree out in front of the tall building. The base of the tree was like a pond, but at this point I didn't care. My baby was dying and nothing mattered anymore. I was sure St. Jude and their doctors were the miracle that God would give Paris and me. I looked down at my feet and saw my stockings were in holes; I must have lost my shoes at some point, and the rain was dripping off my hair.

Some time later that night the doorman came to me, helped me up, and took me up in the elevator to my room. I assured him I was okay and thanked him. Once in the room, I caught a glance of myself in the mirror. Was that me? I looked like a woman who had been hanging on the street corner all night. I was soaked to the skin, what was left of my mascara all over my face. My panty hose were all torn, and I had lost my shoes. I looked worse than a tramp of the night. I looked at myself again more closely in the mirror. I spent time studying the appearance. It was then that I woke up to the reality of what was happening. *This is not a nightmare. My little Paris needs me to think clearly and to deal with what is coming.* I sobered up almost instantly. I got myself out of my wet clothes and into the shower, and I felt better than I had all week. I think it was my acknowledging the facts and coming to some level of acceptance that made me feel that I would cope with everything that was coming. It was as if an inner energy was resonating through me. I couldn't explain it.

One of the many angels dressed in scrubs at St. Jude

I slept fitfully that night and tried to plan in my head how I was going to tell my family and, more important, Paris, the news. How do you tell a little girl that she only has nine months to live? Or should I even tell her at all? But there again was what she told me in the airport lounge in Florida. There was much to do and much to think about.

Chapter 14

JUST BUYING TIME FOR PARIS

The cold morning air felt good as I walked over to the hospital from the hotel. For having been so smashed the night before, I felt amazingly well, with no headache. *What will this day bring? What else is there to consider?*

I met with Mr. Park, and he was as nice as Dr. Steve. He expressed his regret that he and his team could not be more hopeful. The treatment plans were being drawn up to start Paris on several rounds of radiation. It was to be delivered in a way that would protect the rest of her brain as much as possible, allowing her to hold on to her sight, hearing, and ability to think normally for an extended period of time.

Radiation started, and initially Paris had no great side effects. After a few days, she felt nauseated. We were getting used to the routine, but Paris was doing better than I was. She was taking it all in stride, while I was feeling lost and out of place. One minute I was saying to myself, *Deal with it!* Then next minute I was saying, *No, I don't want to deal with it*. I was swinging all day long, and Paris was my greatest support. I was going back into my "is this a bad dream?" mode.

While Paris underwent radiation, I would walk around the hospital, which got me out of the building and helped clear my head for a while. It was on one of my walks that I saw a woman sitting on the grass crying. *Oh, God, what can I say to her?* I just sat down beside this mother and put my arms around her, and she sobbed and sobbed. We didn't really talk too much; she had been told that her little girl's tumor was growing. I could say nothing in response, and she understood that. I guess just having arms around you at that time felt a little comforting, knowing that someone else understood the pain and the helplessness that a mother feels. That's what I missed the most, a shoulder to cry on. But I didn't have one, so I didn't cry but held it inside.

Later that afternoon Paris and I went to the zoo. She enjoyed that, and I could let go of the whole cancer thing for a little while, until the voices in my head reminded me not to get too happy as I had a lot to worry about. Who was this cruel woman in my head, reminding me relentlessly that my baby girl was terminally ill?

Chapter 15

"YOU'VE GOT CANCER TOO, MUMMY!"

One day just merged into another—an endless cycle of radiation, tests, and little sleep—and I was losing track of time. I felt totally lost and had nowhere and no one to turn to for help to save my girl. It was the first time in my life that I felt truly desperate.

It was while Paris was in the bathroom having her shower at our hotel that I fell to my knees and prayed to God like I had never prayed before. I begged him to save my little Paris, to "please give me the cancer" and let her live. For two more days there were trips across the road to St. Jude, each day more painful for me; watching all those little children with their little bald heads was getting to me. I wanted to deny what was happening, but the sight of those little people was branding the word *cancer* into my brain. I was dreading the day I would see Paris bald. I so wanted to escape, but where would I go? There was nowhere to go, I felt as if I were trapped in hell.

We had been living in the hotel across the street from the hospital for almost a week. The room was pleasant with two queen beds. Paris thought it great fun to have a queen bed all to herself. I had often wondered at Paris's happy mood; she pretty much acted as normal, no worries, as if our hotel visit was for a holiday. It would have appeared that Paris didn't have a care in the world. The cancer demon was out of sight and out of her mind, and I was happy with that, because *I* was struggling to hold myself together. What would I have done if she was a basket case like her Mum?

That evening, we both got into our beds. Paris took to a fit of the giggles, which were becoming a frequent occurrence with her. She was rolling about on her big bed, and she giggled so much that I just had to join in with her.

Then she dropped the second bombshell, "You've got cancer too, Mummy!"

"What!"

"You have got cancer!"

Paris was laughing and giggling. My laughter stopped, and then I thought to myself that she must have heard my prayer two nights earlier when she was in the bathroom having her shower, but I was quiet, the heavy bathroom door was closed, and her shower was running—could she really have heard?

"Well, Paris, that is not a funny joke!"

But she still laughed on.

"It's not a joke, you've got cancer; it is in your boob!"

She was still rolling on the bed laughing.

"No, I don't, silly!" I said. "Why would you laugh at something like that?"

"I don't mean to laugh; it just comes out!"

Still her laughing continued.

"Can I come sleep in your bed, Mum?"

"Of course you can."

She jumped into my bed and settled into my arm. Exhausted by laughing, we both lay still and silent for a little while. It was so nice to just cozy up and hold her. Then she said, "It is right there!"

Pointing to the inside of my left breast.

"What is?"

"Your cancer!"

Now she was not laughing and continued, "You have to go and see your doctor."

"Paris, Mummy does not have cancer. Where are you getting all this from? I had my mammogram, and my boobs were checked just three months ago, and all is okay with them!"

Paris burst into tears. She sobbed, "Mummy, you have got cancer, but you're not believing me. You're not paying attention to what I'm saying! I just know! Say you will go to the doctor, please?"

The next day while Paris was having her treatment at the hospital,

I went back across to our hotel room and did a self-examination of my left breast. Nothing felt different than usual. I did have naturally fibrotic breasts, and there was no way of feeling a lump other than what was always there. I sat on the bed and thought *What if my prayer had been answered? What if I did have cancer? That would mean my little girl would be cured, right?* I was a little shaken at the thought of it all.

Paris at home for a weekend break from treatment

I called our family doctor and told her all that had been going on with Paris and Paris's insistence that I too had cancer. My doctor confirmed that my last mammogram of three months ago was as clear as it gets but explained that they can never be 100 percent accurate. She told me that my insurance would not pay for another mammogram so soon and that I would have to pay for another one unless I felt that there was a change in the feeling of my breast that is of concern. Not wanting to take any chances, I made an appointment for a diagnostic mammogram the next week when I returned to Texas with Paris for her weekend off treatment.

Chapter 16

HOME TO TEXAS FOR
THE WEEKEND

I took Paris home every second weekend to see her sister, Helen, and to have just two days to be home and to experience some normal family life since the hotel, as nice as it was, wasn't really home.

I had the diagnostic mammogram late on a Friday evening and was told at that time that it should be no cause for concern. Paris, who insisted in coming along, was waiting for me in the waiting room reading her Harry Potter book. I stepped out to tell her that everything was looking okay, and again she started crying and protesting that the doctor just did not find it. I did not know what to do. I had been going to Dr. Dee for years for my mammograms. Dr. Dee stepped out into the waiting room to see Paris and ask her how she was doing, as she knew of her diagnosis and prognosis. Paris was getting annoyed in a way that I had never seen before and was very emphatic to Dr. Dee, "My Mummy has cancer in her boob!"

This was a very awkward situation, and the doctor felt bad for Paris because she knew she was attending St. Jude and that her cancer was terminal. For Paris's sake, I asked the doctor to please look at the films again, which she did. I was called back in and Dr. Dee said that while she believed all to be well she wanted to do a hands-on exam. She said if anything at all we could do a needle biopsy right where Paris said the location was. The needle biopsy was done, and Dr. Dee said we would have a result first thing Monday morning before Paris and I had to fly back to Memphis to continue Paris's radiation treatment.

Paris, Helen, and I enjoyed our weekend together. The girls spent most of the time cuddled up on the couch together watching TV, and they slept together in the same bed at night. I managed to get several loads of laundry done and get us all repacked.

As expected, I got a call from the doctor's office very early on Monday morning.

"Dr. Dee would like you to come into the office at nine o'clock this morning, Ms. Acree."

"Can't you just give me her message over the phone?"

"No, Ms. Acree, Dr. Dee wants to talk to you in her office."

"Okay, I will be there."

I thought it was a long drive to just talk to Dr. Dee, but I guessed that was how the doctor's office operated. Of course, I expected this to be a routine consultation, laughing to myself that although I had prayed for me to have the cancer, and set my child free, the likelihood of that happening would be one in a billion. But I also knew that God could do one in a billion.

My friend Sue sat with the girls and helped pack the last of our things in our travel bags while I went to meet with Dr. Dee. It took me over an hour to make the twenty-five mile trip in the congested early-morning commuter traffic, but all I was thinking about was laundry. As soon as I walked into the reception area, I was shown to the doctor's office. Dr. Dee always had a warmth about her, and she came from behind her desk and put her arms around me and said, "It's positive; you have a malignant tumor."

I just stood there and looked at her. *Oh my God, Paris was right all along!* Then I remembered my prayer, "Please give me the cancer and let her live." I sat down and tried to process what the doctor was saying to me. I could barely hear her words even though she was sitting right next to me holding my hand. There was a silence that felt very soothing. Dr. Dee remarked that it is rare to have two members of the same family to be diagnosed with cancer within a couple of weeks of each other and that she herself was in disbelief, but that the diagnosis was accurate and that she had already spoken to a top breast cancer surgeon in Austin, whom she highly recommended. The matter had to be taken care of quickly before it spread into my body, she said.

All I could think of was Paris. Could this mean that her tumor was gone? I told the doctor that I had to leave; I had to get home and pick up

Paris and get to the airport. The doctor wanted me to talk with her longer and make plans for my surgery, chemotherapy, and radiation. I told her it all had to wait and that I would call her. With that, I left.

Driving back home, I could not believe what was happening I started to feel elated. God did hear my prayer! The closer I got to home, the more excited I got at just the thought of it. *My baby is going to be okay. My baby girl will live. Thank you, God, thank you, God. After all, that was the deal, right? Give me the cancer and let my child live, right God? I have the cancer.*

I got home in time to load our bags into Sue's car and drive to the airport. We kissed Helen good-bye. I felt torn; I could feel my heart pounding. I could barely wait to get back to St. Jude and have another MRI done on Paris and have the doctors tell me her tumor has gone. My head was reeling, and Paris wanted to know what the doctor had said. I told her the truth, that she was right and that I did have cancer in my breast exactly as she said. She was happy and sad all at the same time. I didn't tell Paris of the bargain I made with God. All she could think of is that we would both get bald together and even wear matching beanie hats. She chattered away the whole trip.

Chapter 17

EXPECTING A MIRACLE

Paris talked nonstop from Austin to Memphis. I don't know if I heard half of what she said; my mind was racing.

"The radiation isn't too bad, Mummy, until the third day, that is, and that is when you will start to feel sick to your stomach, and Dr. Steven is so nice."

Paris had become a little pro in her knowledge of cancer and her treatments, and she kept her doctors going with her endless questions, and they all answered every one.

"I won't be treated at St. Jude's, Paris. St. Jude's is only for children."

I made up my mind that as long as I had the cancer Paris would be free. All I was waiting for was for her to get the all clear. That was as far as my mind could go.

I grabbed Paris's hand and practically dragged her across the parking lot at St. Jude. I couldn't get in the door fast enough. We did our usual check-in and triage; I felt almost nauseated with impatience. We were half an hour early for our appointment with her doctor, and the waiting was killing me.

Paris's name was called, and we made our way to the doctor's office. I hadn't thought of what I was going to tell him.

The doctor began, "Well, how are you feeling, Paris? You look amazing . . ."

"My mummy has cancer too."

What a blurt out!

"What?"

"My mummy has cancer in her boob. Don't you, Mummy!"

The doctor just looked at me in a little bit of disbelief, and he smiled as he asked us to sit down. Then he called for a nurse and asked her to go with Paris for a lemonade, and he handed Paris a few dollars out of his pocket; an amazing man, so relaxed and caring, almost as if the patient in front of him was the only one he had.

Paris left with the nurse and the doctor asked what was going on. The first words out of my mouth were, "Can you please give Paris another MRI. I believe her tumor has gone."

"What has happened over the weekend? Let's talk about you for a minute. Do you have cancer?"

"Yes, I have breast cancer."

"When were you diagnosed?"

"This morning. I had a needle biopsy late Friday."

"I'm so sorry . . ."

I interrupted the doctor and asked again about another MRI for Paris.

"What makes you think Paris's tumor has gone?"

At first I was hesitant to tell him, but at this point I needed to convince him that Paris was healed so that she could get an MRI would prove it.

"I prayed to God a few weeks ago to give me the cancer and let Paris live. God has answered my prayer. I've got the cancer, so I want you to order another MRI and see that Paris's tumor has gone."

I was surprised that the doctor was not easily convinced. Then I was in tears. I didn't want Paris to have her brain blasted with any more radiation when it was no longer needed. I was afraid of the side effects. The doctor was sympathetic but said her next MRI would not be until the end of the week. I was shattered. Still, I just knew all would be well.

The rest of the week dragged by, and Paris attended every day of her radiation therapy. While the doctors did their best to target the radiation beam, they did say that other parts of her brain may possibly be negatively affected, especially her pituitary gland. Still, I had faith that all would be okay.

I did call Dr. Dee back as I said I would. She was insistent that I get back to Austin as soon as possible; she had forwarded my mammography film to the breast surgeon that she highly recommended, Dr. June, and had secured me an early appointment. I got the surgeon's phone number from her and arranged a phone consultation. I could not be at two places at the same time, and I needed to be with Paris. I took a deep breath and called the number.

The receptionist said that she really wanted me to come into the office as soon as possible. I explained that I was out of state but did agree to set up an initial consultation call with Dr. June later in the afternoon. All I knew was that I had breast cancer; I didn't know that there were different cancer cell types, and at that point I didn't care too much. Paris was my only focus.

I made the call back to Dr. June's office as planned.

"How soon can you come in, Ms. Acree? I got your film from Dr. Dee's office."

I told her that I was in Tennessee with Paris and that I could not be there anytime soon as I had to wait on Paris's MRI at the end of the week.

"Ms. Acree, your condition is urgent and we do need to meet right away!"

How could I tell her about my deal with God?

"Just as soon as I get back to Austin, I will come, but right now I need to be with my little girl. Thank you so much I will call you back."

With that, I hung up. I must have sounded ungrateful, but I needed Thursday to come to see that Paris was going to be all right, and I knew that wouldn't make sense to anyone else. Thursday afternoon the nurse informed me that Paris would be scheduled for an MRI in the morning. I was thrilled; at last I would hear the words "Paris's tumor is gone." Then we could celebrate. Was I being overly presumptuous? No. I had made my deal with God, and I had faith in him. I must surely have been the only woman in the world to be so happy to have cancer.

Paris and I went out to a nice restaurant that evening and pigged out on the desserts. Normally we had eaten a strict diet of organic foods since Paris's diagnosis, but I wanted to celebrate. I made up my mind that I was not going to say anything to Paris about the miracle that was about to be discovered; I wanted her to hear it straight from her doctor.

I spent the remainder of the evening listening to Paris's endless chatter. For the first time in a long time I laughed with her endless giggles. In the evening I bathed her in a bubble bath as a special treat and shampooed her silky brown hair. While doing so, I could see the large bald area where her radiation therapy had taken its toll, but I knew it would grow in again over time.

Paris read to me that night from Harry Potter. She enjoyed reading and was making sure I was paying attention. We said our prayers, each taking our turns. I gave a silent prayer to God, thanking him for the miracle that would soon be announced.

I cuddled with Paris until she fell asleep. I couldn't see her face clearly, so I wiggled my arm from underneath her. I knelt at the side of her bed and just looked at her. She looked so peaceful as she slept, and I found myself smiling and thanking God.

The lights were out, and I opened the curtains of our hotel room. I often sought solace in the night sky. It didn't matter if the sky was over Memphis, Tennessee; Albuquerque, New Mexico; Japan; or Scotland—it was all the same wonderment to me, and it brought me some peace. I did go to bed eventually, but I tossed and turned most of the night, always looking at the clock, whose hand moved slowly.

It was morning and a day of miracles for me. We both got dressed and went downstairs for breakfast. Paris polished off a plate of pancakes and some orange juice. I was too nervous to eat anything. Across the street at the hospital again, I resumed my pacing while Paris was taken away for her MRI. It had become my only physical activity, and I think I had paced a hundred miles or more over the last month.

When I finally saw Paris hurrying down the corridor to meet me, she was all smiles, and I thought maybe the doctor had already told her of the miracle; my heart was pounding so hard that I could hear it in my ears, and everything else was silent.

The nurse was a few paces behind Paris, and she too was smiling, but there again she always had a smile in her face.

"Paris did a good job this morning, and Dr. Steve will meet with you in a bit to go over Paris's films with you—"

I cut the nurse off and said, "But it has gone, hasn't it?"

Then I saw Dr. Steve coming our way and I rushed up to him.

"Oh, Dr. Steve, it has gone, hasn't it?"

"Come with me and let's look at Paris's films together."

I had no problem keeping pace with Dr. Steve; I could not get to his office fast enough.

"These are Paris's films from two weeks ago, and here is the tumor . . ."

Over the past few weeks I had become familiar with what I was looking at on the films.

". . . and these are her films from today."

"But it is still there and it looks bigger than the last one? How can this be? What are you saying to me?"

I felt sick to my stomach.

"I'm so sorry, but Paris's tumor is growing not only in size but in density."

I just could not believe what he was saying to me.

"There has to be a mistake. I prayed for the cancer, and I've got it. I asked God for it; it was a deal!"

I was becoming a basket case. The doctor was talking to me, and I could see his lips moving, but I didn't hear another word. My world suddenly became silent and still. Without having to think it through, it came to me that I was trying to make a deal with God, but he did not agree to any deal with me. He just gave me the cancer I prayed for, and that is where the deal ended.

I left the doctor's office and glided down the corridor to Paris—as always she was smiling. I took her hand, and we walked together across the street to the hotel. Of course I was mindful of the traffic, looking both ways and waiting for a safe opening in the stream of traffic to cross, but I could not hear any noise, almost as if I were deaf. My periods of deafness were becoming more frequent; each time it was like a painkiller, so soothing.

We made it to the hotel room, and I locked the door behind us. I don't know if all my door-locking was to lock us in or to lock the world out. I handed Paris the remote control for the television and went into the bathroom. I sat on the commode, and all I could hear was silence. I stared at the towels on the rail in front of me and fingered them, feeling their texture; they were soft to the touch. I looked up at the light in the ceiling and noticed that there were dead flies in it.

I started to hear a banging noise somewhere far off in the distance; the bathroom door opened, and it was Paris.

"I'm hungry, Mum!"

It took me a minute or two to understand what she had said to me. I came out of the bathroom, and the room was in darkness except for the light from the television. I put on the lights and closed the blinds. I don't know how long I had been in the bathroom.

"Okay, let's order in. You pick anything you want!"

"What about my special diet?"

"Paris, you can have anything you want!"

"Cheese pizza, please!"

"Then cheese pizza it is, sweetheart."

We had our usual bedtime routine that evening, with one exception: I did not say any prayers. I was angry with God.

Chapter 18

SIX MONTHS TO LIVE

The next week went by in a blur. I missed the family life that the girls and I'd had. We had been a happy little family of three, and all had been well in our world. We had been so looking forward to having our house built, with a big backyard, and possibly growing a vegetable garden and fruit trees. Both the girls were doing well in school and getting good grades with the intention that they would one day go on to college. I got a late start on my higher education but was working toward my bachelor's degree. We had plans, we had goals, we had dreams, and now . . . who knows. All this cancer was never a part of the plan; feelings of resentment and anger were growing in me.

Paris and I were due to go home to Texas for the weekend. Paris had missed Helen so much and I did too; making phone calls to her was not the same as being with her and tucking her into bed each night. She was my little girl too, and she was so excited about being ten now.

I met with Dr. June in Austin, and she was quite emphatic about telling me the state of my own cancer diagnosis. I still wanted to hold off and keep my cancer, thinking that God would still work the miracle. Bottom line, the doctor thought I was being foolish and told me straight that without immediate surgery and treatment I would have about six months to live.

It was all beginning to sound like some sick joke to me. Paris gets a nine-month sentence and I get a six. That is what it felt like . . . life sentences.

Paris, more than once, brought up my cancer, and I always changed the subject. She would speak so freely about both our conditions as if we each had a case of the measles.

Over the years I'd had my share of pain, especially the loss of my brother. At that time I thought that the pain of his suicide would be the worst experience I would ever have to suffer; never for a moment did I think I would lose a child. Now I had cancer too. What was going to happen to Helen? Was this all bad luck or was I being punished for something? I was trying to make sense of it all but couldn't.

Chapter 19

PARIS THE GUINEA PIG

Paris fully participated in all her treatment therapy and was suited up and allowed into the St. Jude Children's Research Hospital's laboratory. This excited her to no end.

"I got to see my cancer cells, Mum!"

Oh, good grief. She never gives up! There were times I wanted to say "no more" to her with all her happy upbeat attitudes. The truth was I needed to console her as a mother should, but Paris didn't need consoling. Or maybe I was the one who needed the consoling; having a shoulder to lean on would have been nice, but I had no one. Most likely if there had been, I may have pushed it away. Over time I knew this was to be my own Gethsemane; something was telling me that this was something I needed to experience. It was all senseless to me, but I had no choice but to go along with everything that was happening.

Paris had become good buddies with phenomenal doctors. She asked them endless questions about cancer, and she enjoyed telling me all about it. Sometimes it was as if Paris was talking about some science project instead of her own life. I didn't want to know and was quick to change the subject.

Paris told me of another treatment that the doctors were developing in their research center: "It is a new drug, Mum, and they need some patients to try it. It is called a protocol, and I want to try it"

"Paris, the new drug won't help you."

"I know, Mum, but it will help find answers and I want to do it."

As usual, I changed the subject. When we had our next meeting with the doctors, Paris took a paper from the doctor's hand and gave it to me.

"You need to sign this, Mum."

The form was to give permission for Paris to participate in a new drug trial. This new drug would do nothing for Paris at all, except to make her sick each day, so I said no.

"Mum, this is what I want to do. I know it won't help me. It's for research. It's not fair, because I'm a kid I don't get to choose. I want to do it, Mum"

In my heart of hearts I knew that Paris knew that she was not going to survive her cancer. I had to recognize that at her age, now nine and a half, she had a right to make her choices during what little time she had left. Something else was going on here, and I couldn't quite put my finger on it. Somewhere over the past few months Paris had acquired a greater understanding of her situation and the grand scheme of life. In many ways she was right, I had to pay attention. In time, I signed the form for her, and she was elated. Paris did take part in a new trial. She took pleasure in calling herself a guinea pig; she thought it was good fun. For doing this, Paris's name was engraved on a plaque and hung on the wall outside St. Jude's laboratory center.

Chapter 20

THE NEW HOUSE IS BUILT

Between treatment cycles, Paris and I returned to Texas several times, and each time we visited the house builder and interior design department. I had originally put a hold on construction because I did not know what was going to happen with my family. I explained that I was out of state a lot and why. The builder was so accommodating and said all we had to do was pick the floor plan and colors, and they would do their best to have the house completed in ten weeks and in time for Paris to come home. They kept to their word; they worked on the house seven days a week until it was completed.

Chapter 21

LUMPECTOMY

As Paris's tumor grew, it was time for me to decide what to do about my own cancer, which was a heartbreaking decision. While I would gladly have given my life to save Paris's, it was not to be. I couldn't do anything to halt or cure her cancer and its growing density. I knew it was still possible for Paris to outlive me, but it was as if she was reading my mind.

"Mum, I want you to hold me when I die."

Those words crushed my heart. I also knew that I still had Helen to raise and needed to be there for her as best as I was able.

I went ahead and had a lumpectomy, and clean margins ensured that my entire tumor was removed. While I should have been elated at such a result, I had deep feelings of guilt that were becoming increasingly hard to live with. Knowing that I was going to live and Paris would die was a pain that was to haunt me for many years. Why couldn't they have saved my baby instead? Why did God not hear me? Or maybe he did and ignored me, or maybe, or maybe . . . or maybe what? I had no answers.

Chapter 22

DISNEY WORLD FOR PARIS AND HELEN

Our small family, including the girls' dad, got to take a trip to Disney World, a gift from the Make-A-Wish Foundation. While Paris could have chosen to visit the pyramids or go on a world cruise, she chose to go to Disney World

"Because I think Helen will really like it, Mum." Paris was thinking of Helen as she made her choice.

Sitting on the plane, I enjoyed watching the faces of my two girls in their excitement at going to the theme park of every little girl's dream. The taxi driver that I mercilessly spat at on the way to St. Jude would have been right if he were to have been the cab driver who picked us up this morning. After everything we'd been through, we were going to Disney World!

I bought Helen and Paris the full Cinderella outfits, including the tiaras and glass slippers, which they both just loved. How they both danced and laughed all week. While Helen and I stayed away from the more wild rides, Paris and her dad rode on every attraction in the park.

I had made my mind up ahead of time that I would be cheerful, but my intentions didn't work out as planned. I appeared happy on the out-side to see the girls having fun, but I had feelings of bitterness and resent-ment. It amazed me that, while Paris knew she would pass on, she never mentioned cancer at all. She behaved like any healthy little girl would at the dream park.

I felt I was a faker, walking around "acting" the part of a happy mum with my children and husband, when in fact, he was my former husband, and one of my little girls was terminally ill. I wondered if we looked normal to others, or if I put on a good show.

Despite the painful undercurrent of the reason Paris had received this wonderful gift, our week at Disney World was a blast for the girls.

Chapter 23

TRANSCENDENTAL MEDITATION

In the early summer of 2000, Paris said, "I want to go home now, Mum, and be with Helen."

Paris, having completed her treatments and her "guinea pig" project, was ready to let go of her cancer identity. The medical staff at St. Jude had given Paris all cancer treatments that they possibly could, but to no avail; all that gave us was a little more time. Her wishes were honored, and we came home to our new house.

Paris and I returned to Texas to try the best we could to have some normalcy. Helen was so happy to have her mum and her sister back home for good. Paris appeared well and attended school and picked up her grades where she had left off. But there was a difference in our home. We were always aware of the uninvited guest, but we dealt with it as best we could.

I had several follow-ups with the breast surgeon, who always assured me that my prognosis was "wonderful, cancer free, and doing great." The inner anguish of knowing I was surviving but losing my child had become an unbearable guilt in my heart. I thought my pain had bottomed out, yet by each passing day it only got worse.

"How deep does this pain get?" I would ask myself in the bathroom mirror; it was a bottomless pit of guilt, despair—a living hell.

I was a member of a local chapter of Toastmasters' International, a public-speaking group, and the members were such warm people, always encouraging and always supportive. Since Paris's diagnosis and mine, the membership had become like family to me and my small family. It was there that I met a wonderful woman by the name of Sais Bagnola, who felt it would be good for me to meet her husband, Jim, who was a Transcendental Meditation instructor.

I was later invited to a party at the Bagnola home, which was located within a spiritual community on the southwest edge of Austin, Texas. There I met so many truly amazing people who all had one thing in common: they were all practitioners of Transcendental Meditation (TM). It was then that I was introduced to Sais's husband, Jim.

Initially I found Jim to be charismatic but soon realized that this was his healthy self-confidence. It was obvious to me that Jim was a centered man and knew who he was and what he was about. Jim was sure of himself; he was an international speaker and lecturer in the human potential arena, and his only agenda was to assist others in their business and personal progress.

Jim found time at the party to have a little one-on-one conversation with me where he spoke to me about the benefits of Transcendental Meditation, more often referred to as TM. Jim invited me to bring my young daughters with me at a future date and to learn the art and benefits of the practice of TM.

When the day came, Paris and Helen were excited to meet Jim. He had a sense of humor that any child could understand; he could take on the personality of a circus clown when he wanted to, and he quickly put my girls at ease. The TM lectures and instructions were underway. Instruction was given to sit upright in a comfortable chair with eyes closed. In silence we were to silently repeat to ourselves a generic mantra. This meditation should ideally last for twenty minutes and be done twice a day. During meditation, there is an opportunity to allow pain to come up out of the past and to simply let go of its negative energy. The continued practice over time brings about peacefulness. My girls, especially Paris, grasped the concepts.

On the final day of instruction, our personal mantras were given to us. The mantra that is given is sacred and not shared with others. With faithful use, over time I could experience silence and peace; this is exactly what I needed. I used TM, rightly—or wrongly—to escape the now growing madness of my mind and its endless chatter. But as time went on, I couldn't ignore that Paris was wasting away and I gave up the practice, feeling defeated.

More than once I walked into Paris's bedroom to find her meditating; she took it all quite seriously and took up the position and posture of the many yogis that she had seen. I didn't inquire how she was progressing because it seemed to be something very personal to her.

I could never tell just how much Transcendental Meditation helped Paris cope, but I did witness, among many other things, that she was at peace with all that was happening, both within herself and around her. Despite all she was going through, having full awareness that her cancer was terminal, Paris still smiled quite naturally.

It was in the fall of 2000 that I started to notice the paralysis in Paris, and it broke my heart to witness it. We celebrated her tenth birthday several months later and Helen had turned eleven the month before, but they were bittersweet occasions, knowing as we did that they'd be some of the last birthdays we'd enjoy together as a family.

Chapter 24

"YOU CAN ONLY GET A NINE OUT OF TEN, MUMMY!"

As my psychological well-being was diminishing, I had not realized just how much I had neglected my personal appearance and regular hygiene maintenance. I just didn't care anymore; my feelings of guilt were engulfing me, and merely getting through the day and night was a struggle.

As time went on, Paris's paralysis got worse. It had started with her inability to hold her spoon; she kept dropping it to the floor, and she would just laugh while I died a little inside as I watched her slowly losing her physical faculties. She started to drag her leg as she walked until she just started hopping; this too was funny to her. Not only was her ever-growing paralysis crushing me, but her laughing at it all just added to my pain.

The thing that broke my heart the most was to see her pretty little face become so distorted with the ever-increasing paralysis that affected the left side of her body. At one point, I covered the bottom half of the vanity mirror in her bathroom so she would not be hurt by her appearance. Paris was quite insistent that I clean off the mirror because seeing her face was okay with her; she even found her sight of her paralyzed face a source of amusement. The time soon came when she could no longer walk. Like most mothers of young girls, I used to watch as Paris attended ballet and tap dancing classes as well as gymnastics. Now all I could see her do was crawl on the floor; Paris found humor in this also, calling herself "the friendly caterpillar." I would cringe at such remarks, and I was slowly reverting into a hole of despair.

Paris remarked one morning, "Mum, are you okay?"

I lied, "I'm okay, why?"

"Well you don't wear any of your Gucci skirts anymore, and you never wear any makeup now."

Looking at my appearance in the mirror, I saw Paris was right. I looked a mess. I would wear the same old sweats for days on end and forget to bathe. My body had become riddled in pain, and it was hard to dress, and the feeling of running water on my skin was becoming excruciatingly painful. I had developed toothaches and earaches and pounding headaches. My worst condition was the guilt I felt every waking moment, knowing my breast cancer had been removed by a lumpectomy and multiple rounds of radiation. I got to live, only to watch my daughter die. I was engulfed by feelings and thoughts of guilt. Paris had so much more to offer the world than I did. God only gave me half of my prayer: he gave me the cancer but didn't take Paris's away. Why would he do that?

After looking in the mirror, I realized my shabby appearance would be the last memory that Paris would have of me, and I didn't want that. I was determined not to let her down. She deserved better than I had been giving her.

I woke the next morning from a fitful night's sleep on the couch and wandered into my bathroom. As hard and painful as it was, I bathed and dressed, wearing a nice skirt and blouse, and did the best I could with my hair and makeup. I decided to treat Paris like a princess that morning by bringing a breakfast tray to her. I made the tray look as pretty as I could and went into the garden to cut a pink rose from the rose bushes that grew outside her bedroom window.

I was really pleased with my efforts and walked into her bedroom with the tray and my "new" appearance. I had walked in on Paris as she was sitting perfectly still doing her meditation. Paris was better at it than I was. My mind was too busy, and I never seemed to be able to quiet it. Paris, however, was faithful to the practice.

Paris was delighted with the breakfast surprise and said, "Five out of ten!"

"Really, Paris, only five out of ten?"

She started her usual giggling, and I felt a little disappointed.

"I liked my breakfast, and I love the pink rose, but I love yellow ones better. And you look nicer in a dress."

It was not like Paris to talk to me in this way, and I got a bit bent out of shape. I thought I made a great effort, and I only got a five out of ten!

The next morning, I bathed and dressed in a pretty summer dress and plucked a yellow rose for her breakfast tray. We had only two rose bushes in the front garden, a pink one and a yellow one. Helen and Paris brought the young bushes back from a road trip to Tyler, Texas, the year previously, and they were now mature enough to give many roses.

I thought I looked quite nice, and her breakfast tray was pretty with the yellow rose. I entered her bedroom, and she was there with her smile and cuddly elephant. She started her usual giggle routine.

"Okay, princess, what are you giggling about?"

"I'm not giggling, Mum, but I need to do my meditation first before I eat."

Paris had often denied giggling when she was in fact giggling. There was something different about her; she was more adamant in things she said, and sometimes I would think she was being rude and a little outspoken to her mother. It was humbling to have to admit to myself that my child, the one who was terminally ill, was taking the lead. I was beginning to feel inadequate both as a mother and a person.

"Seven out of ten!"

I didn't know if Paris really thought I was only a "seven out of ten" or if she was just playing a game with me. I tried not to let my disappointment show. Game or not, I was starting to take this all too seriously.

This morning routine would repeat itself for several days. I learned not to go into her room too early as her mediation time was important to her. I had gotten to a score of eight out of ten, and I was now taking it very personally. I wanted Paris to think of me as a great mother, but my score was only moving up incrementally over a few days. I knew time was running out for Paris, and I wanted to make sure I was going to get my ten; this had become very important to me.

That evening, once Helen and Paris were asleep, I dug into the back of my closet and found a turquoise-blue sequined cocktail dress. It was beautiful. I had bought it for a special occasion a few years earlier that never took place, and I had never worn it. Paris had often asked if she could have it for dress-ups with Helen. I always said no as it had been an expensive dress and that I hoped to have a special occasion to wear it someday. I hung the dress on the door, ready for the morning.

Getting my ten was consuming me; I wanted my little girl to give me a ten out of ten for being her mum, and I would get a lump in my throat at the thought of getting a lower score.

My big morning had arrived and I was up early to get bathed, curl my hair, and get my face made up; this took some time because I was in constant pain. I found high-heeled shoes that would go perfectly with the dress. Breakfast was set on the lap-table along with not one but three yellow roses. One more look in the mirror and the game was on; there was no way I would not get my ten that morning.

I was polite enough to knock on Paris's bedroom door.

"Come in!"

I had my smile on!

"How is Princess Paris this morning?"

Paris gave out all the usual giggles and laughter, "She is well!"

Paris ate her breakfast with a little help. She tried her best to pick up the yellow roses, so I held them to her nose. She gave a big smile. I was waiting for her to tell me that I got a score of ten out of ten, but she said nothing. So I stood up and gave a twirl.

"What do you think?"

"You are so pretty, Mummy!"

"Thank you, Princess Paris."

But that is all that she said; she never gave me a score. So I made small talk while my score was going on in my head. Still she did not mention my score, so I asked, "So, I get a ten out of ten this morning?"

"No, you get a nine."

Paris was not smiling or giggling. She was serious, and I was hurt. Paris did not know how important it was to me, as her mother, that I get a perfect ten; less than ten would mean that I had failed her. My guilt of having survived her was gripping me. I wondered if Paris felt it was unfair, but I did not dare ask her. The lump in my throat got bigger.

"Paris, I'm so sorry that I have not been the best mum in the world, but could you tell me what I have to do to get a ten out of ten? I can't think of anything else to do!"

In her slurred speech she said, "You are the best mummy in the world, but you can only get a nine out of ten."

Paris was in a state of giggles again. I didn't think it was so funny.

"If you get a ten, you will think it is okay to stop growing; with a nine you have space to grow."

Paris's remark left me speechless. I excused myself and went into my bathroom and sat on the edge of my tub.

What had she just said to me? I sat there and repeated her words to myself out loud. I gave it a bit of thought. That was quite a remark to come from a child. But did it matter that she was just a child; did it make the message less meaningful?

Paris often said things in her giggles that would catch my attention. As smart as Paris was, this was a whole new genre. There was something more to her attitude than I could grasp.

Chapter 25

THE LAST VALENTINE'S DAY

Our morning started out as usual. Sue picked up Helen to take her to school. Paris and I were going to have breakfast.

"Okay, Paris, what do you feel like having this morning?"

"I'll have brownies and ice cream!"

"What? Since when do we have dessert for breakfast?"

Paris went into a fit of laughter, and I could not help but notice the great paralysis in her little face. It broke my heart but I managed to look beyond and see the sparkle in her beautiful eyes.

"I'm dying, Mummy! She laughed. "It doesn't matter what I eat!"

I was startled by what she had just said. She was right of course; healthy diet was no longer an issue, but I was taken aback with her laughter and attitude. She knew she would die soon and all she could do was laugh and want brownies and ice cream for breakfast! Well, why not— brownies and ice cream it was! We sat on the couch together, and I joined her in having dessert for breakfast. She managed to feed herself but struggled. She had more breakfast on her pajamas than she could get in her mouth, but no matter.

While Paris did her best with the remaining brownies, I ran a bath for her. She was down to the last of enjoyments; she had by now lost most of her peripheral vision and was no longer able to read, and she had lost her ability to crawl and wiggle on the floor to get around, so bath time was her only fun time. I added scented bubbles and got hot towels out of the dryer and clean clothes ready.

I went to pick Paris up off the couch when I saw that she was in tears;

93

even with everything she'd gone through, she rarely cried. I just sat with her on my lap and held her close.

"Talk to me, Paris"

What do you say to your ten-year-old who knows she will die soon as she cries? What does a mother say or ask? Then she blew me away when she said, "I just don't want you to forget me, Mummy!"

I just sat her on my knee like the baby she was to me and held her tightly, and we wept together for a while; they were the first tears I had shed in a long time.

"Paris, I will never forget you! Tell you what: every year on your birthday, we will still have birthday cake for you! I will never ever forget you, do you hear me, do you understand me!"

I was at a loss for anything else to say. I hurriedly added more hot water to her bath, then got her into the bathroom. She looked around the bathroom as well as she could with what little tunnel vision she had left. Upon looking at her clean clothes that I picked out for her, she said, "I think I want to wear the pretty pink pajamas today"

Weeks previously Paris had seen a pair of pink pajamas trimmed with lace, and we bought them. But whenever I asked that she wear them she would say no, that she was keeping them for a "special day"—the day she was going to die. I found that a bit morbid, but Paris was comfortable talking about death and more especially her own. I, not so much!

"I thought you were keeping those pj's special?"

"I was, but I think it is okay to wear them today."

How totally stupid was I not to catch that? She was telling me something, and I was not paying close enough attention. The bath time went well, despite my struggle to hold her body weight and shampoo and bathe her at the same time. Paris, however, was giggling at my lame attempt to hold her now paralyzed body. We had some splash time, almost as if she were an infant again. Between the two of us, we completed that bath, and I carried her little wet body through to her bedroom and placed her on the warm towel that I had spread on her bed. We laughed and cuddled her dry. I dressed Paris in the pink lace-trimmed pajamas as she wanted, and I blow-dried her hair in the bob style that she wore so well. Paris had purple nail polish on her toes, and I suggested we remove it as it was looking a bit worn, but she said, "No, I want to shock Jesus. Just wait till he sees my toes!"

She was in a fit of giggles again. Paris never ceased to surprise me with some of the things she would say.

"So you think this nail polish will be okay with Jesus, do you?"

"He is funny. He will like it!"

Her sense of humor about the subject of her own death was astounding. We had previously bought Paris a beautiful gown by Jessica McClintock; it was pale cream and long. I remember the day we bought it; she tried it on and loved it. Yes, it was expensive, but I knew I would never buy her a wedding gown. The sales assistant, poor girl, suggested that the store could have the dress shortened a little, but Paris was quick to interject with giggles and said, "I won't need to have is shortened. I won't be walking in it; this dress is for when I go to meet Jesus when I die!"

Paris had the biggest smile on her face; you would have thought she was going to a wedding. The sales assistant looked shocked as she glanced at me. I just nodded. We also picked out pretty socks trimmed with lace and little white lace-covered slippers. Paris was so happy with her new outfit, all to meet Jesus, she insisted.

The hospice nurse had visited a few days previously and said that Paris was declining and had about a week to go. Paris, for some reason, did not like the nurse's visits; she said it was just a lot of fuss.

I was about to carry her through to the living room and prop her up on the couch as I had been doing. We would cuddle up together and watch *Little House on the Prairie* on TV, but she wanted to be in her bed. This was the first time Paris had asked to stay in bed. She was quite talkative in her own way; the paralysis had affected her speech, but she made herself understood and sometimes used hand signs. Thumbs-up was for yes and thumbs-down for no. Next to Paris's bed was a gift of a tiny teddy bear pin fashioned like an angel. I pinned it on her pink lace pajamas, and she smiled. Her favorite cuddly toy had become a gray elephant, which she called Elvis, a gift from her schoolteacher. I played *The Little Princess* on the tape player for her as she was no longer able to read. She seemed to be content and fell asleep after a while.

I went into the kitchen and cleaned up, then did some laundry. I peeked in Paris's room. She was awake and had to turn her head all the way around to see me with her tunnel vision. She started one of her giggling fits, and I had to just laugh with her. She wanted to know what time it was and if Helen was home from school yet. No. Five minutes later she would ask again.

"Don't worry. Helen will be right in to see you as soon as she comes home."

"I hope that maybe some of my school friends got cards for me and that they will give them to Helen for me!"

Valentine's Day, I had forgotten. Each day seemed to be so alike, they merged into one; often I didn't know what day of the week it was. Before we knew it, Helen came bounding in the door, straight into Paris's bedroom with a very large bag.

"Look, Paris, just about everybody in school sent you a Valentine's card!"

Paris soon perked up and struggled to sit up. We propped her up with pillows, and she started digging in the bag. There were many small packages of candy and chocolate. But she was more interested in the cards. It brought tears to my eyes to see her struggle to read, so Helen and I read all of them to her. With each card she smiled and hugged each card. She was so thrilled with all the cards she got, especially the ones from the boys.

Exhausted, Paris lay back on her pillows. She had the biggest smile on her face. She had been waiting all day for her cards, and I'm so glad that all her school friends had made such a fuss over her; they had brought so much happiness to my little girl.

I asked Paris if she wanted to come sit on the couch while I made dinner, but she didn't want to; she said she wanted to just stay cozy in bed. She and Helen had fun looking through all the cards, and I went into the kitchen.

I dished up dinner for Helen, and as she ate, I went into Paris's bedroom. She was lying motionless in her bed, Valentines all over the bed. I asked her if she could hear me, but I thought she was asleep. She was breathing, but with a slight raspy sound. This was different; I had not heard this raspy sound before, so I shook her gently. At first she did not respond, but then she was wide-eyed and asked what I wanted.

"I can see you, Mummy, really see you!"

My heart started pumping. I knew something was going on, something changing. I just held her, rocked her, then she said, "Oh, I can't see too well now."

The raspy sound of her breathing remained after she woke up, as if she was struggling to breathe. Then it hit me. She wanted to wear the pretty pink pajamas and said she wanted to keep the purple nail polish on her toes to shock Jesus. *Oh my heavens!* I knew it was all about to happen. *Why didn't I pick up on it? The nurse said a week! The week isn't up yet!*

Paris was comfortable, and I had a sense that she was not going to pass in her sleep. The time had come. I called Paris and Helen's father to come get Helen. I didn't want Helen to be afraid, and I didn't know how it was going to be. Weeks before, we already agreed that there would be "no resuscitation" and Paris did not want doctors or nurses around and wanted to die at home, in her own bed.

"Just you and me, Mummy, okay? Promise you will be with me when I die, promise?"

"I promise, Paris, you and me, baby."

She knew, and she had known since this morning. That's why she wanted to stay in bed. I bet that she was hanging in there for those Valentine's Day cards. Strange what will make a body hang in there a little bit longer. Where was my head? My baby was dying! I didn't say anything to Helen except to come sit with her little sister and give her hugs and kisses. I went to the phone and had their father come to take Helen for the night. He did, and he too kissed Paris for the last time and left with Helen.

Chapter 26

PARIS TAKES
HER LAST BREATH

After having given Paris many hugs and kisses, Helen left with her father, and Paris and I were alone, and the house had become very peaceful. Paris napped on and off throughout the evening; I was afraid to leave her side, never knowing if she would wake up from each nap. But as she did so, I put my hand in hers, and she would give a little squeeze and a weak smile.

By midnight Paris had become restless. She hadn't eaten for over twelve hours and didn't want anything to drink. I called the hospice nurse and told her that Paris did not want any water and that she was very restless. The nurse explained that as the end nears the body does not want food or water. She offered to come to the house, but I said no, as Paris just wanted the two of us. *This is it. The end is nearing. God, give me strength to get through the night.*

I sat on the edge of Paris's bed and took her pulse. It was a little fast, her hands were warm, and she was talking to me the best she could in her slurred speech, "I'm okay, Mummy, not to worry."

Then the giggling started again, it was coming from her tummy and she was smiling and then she closed her eyes. She was still breathing and appeared to be asleep. Each time she dozed off, I wondered if that would be for the last time. The raspiness of her breathing was still there and sounded as if it was getting stronger and louder. This continued throughout the night. I could hear her heart beating as I sat on her bed. The noise was eerie, just a continuous thumping, and it got faster and louder. It scared me. The hours dragged on, and Paris's breathing was becoming more labored; she was struggling with every breath.

I left her bedroom to turn off the heating and turn on the air-conditioning to cool her room, but the room just got hotter. I had already pulled back her bed covers and I removed most of my own clothes too. I stood on the end of her bed to put my hand up to the air vent on the ceiling and I could feel cold air at the vent, but no cold air was coming down into the room. I ran through the house, opening all the windows, including the window in the bedroom; the rest of the house was cold, but Paris's bedroom was like an oven.

At one point Paris did open her eyes again; I got up close almost nose to nose. I told her whatever I thought would help her with her struggle.

"Can you hear me, Paris?"

I held her hand and she gave a weak thumbs-up. She could still hear me, but for how long?

Suddenly Paris would start to shake uncontrollably. At one point I thought her small body would bounce off her bed.

Paris was now moving erratically on the bed so much so that I climbed on the bed and straddled her to stop her from falling off and onto the floor.

The heat in the room was becoming unbearable, yet I was mindful that Paris wanted to die in her own bed. I wrapped a sheet across Paris and tucked it in until I could race to the kitchen to get some ice water and washcloths for us both.

As I went to the door of her bedroom, it appeared to be concaved, bowed outward like the door of an airplane. Even more strange, the corner of the wall at the door was smoothed out as if there was no corner at all, though I didn't have time to wonder about it.

In the kitchen I grabbed a large jug and filled it with ice and water and got some clean kitchen towels. I could hear the sound of her thumping heart beating as I stood at the refrigerator; it had gone from a thumping to a clunking sound, almost echoing. I was a wreck, frantically trying to get everything and get back to my baby.

Back in the bedroom, I pulled the sheet off Paris and straddled her again to stop her from falling off the bed.

I bathed her with the cold wet cloths and rubbed her lips with ice to cool her off. I soaked myself with the wet cloths as the heat in the room intensified. It was killing me inside to watch my child struggling to breathe; I knew she needed to let go now. I cradled her in my arms like the baby she was to me.

"Paris, it's okay to let go now, sweetheart. Go be with Jesus and let him see your purple toes. You will see my Nana and Uncle Benny too! It will be all okay, you wait and see! Let go, Paris. I will always love you, and Helen will always love you, and we will never ever forget you. Remember, we will have birthday cake for you every birthday. Did you hear me, Paris?"

There was another thumbs-up. It was weak but unmistakably a thumbs-up—she had heard me. Her beautiful eyes closed for the last time. I thought for sure that she would pass at that point, but she did not.

Nothing left to do, I pulled Paris up to my chest and continued to straddle her to keep her from falling off the bed. The loud rasping of her breathing and the loud clucking of her heart was killing me. I felt that for the total of all the wrong things I ever did in my life, I was now paying the price for it all. I held her close and rocked her back and forth. To God, who everyone says will not give you more than you can handle, I made it clear that I felt quite strongly he was being merciless to my dying child.

"Take her! God, take her now! Why are you letting her go on like this? She is ready to go! Please don't let my baby suffer any longer! Take her!"

As I screamed to God, I held Paris close to my chest and rocked her back and forth.

As I did so, I noticed that the wall behind the headboard of her bed curved onto the ceiling; as I looked around the room, there were no corners, as if we were inside a ball. I thought I was going out of my mind. Her thumping heart, the loud rasping as she slowly suffocated, and the room was now a ball. I was in a nightmare. Then pop! I felt it hit my chest! The rasping had stopped as Paris exhaled for the last time. It was like a slow whisper, and I could feel it on my skin. I just kept on rocking her so tight. I knew she was gone, but I was afraid to let her go.

I rocked Paris until I realized I was very cold. The cold February night air was blowing in the window and the air-conditioning was running full blast, which I could feel blowing cold on my back. I leaned forward and laid Paris's head on her pillow. I was overjoyed as I looked at her little face; all the signs of paralysis were gone. Her face was perfectly shaped and looked as though she had a slight smile on it. The cold drove me to get off the bed and close the window and grab my clothes and dress. Then I ran through the house to turn off the air-conditioning, close all the windows, and turn on the heating.

It was four something on the clock, but I don't know exactly the minute of Paris's death. I called the hospice number and spoke with the nurse. I asked her to give me an hour with Paris as I wanted to bathe and dress her myself. I sponge-bathed her and dressed her in her cream Jessica McClintock gown. I was so tempted to remove the purple nail polish from her toes, but smiled and thought, *No. Paris will have her wish.* I did not put on the frilly socks and lace–covered slippers either—just to make sure that Paris would "shock Jesus" as she said she would. By the time I had finished with her, she looked beautiful, like a porcelain doll. It was then that I noticed that her bedroom had become square again; the ball-shaped room had disappeared. The hospice nurse came in and checked Paris over and gave her a time of death 5:10 a.m.

Paris left home for the last time at 7:30 a.m. that morning. It was a strange feeling. Paris was adamant that she be cremated and not buried. And that she was to be cremated the same day as her death. That was not the legal way in the state of Texas, but our family physician pleaded our case that her death was of a natural cause. Imagine that, cancer as a natural cause of death. Still, Paris had her wish, and she was cremated at 2:00 p.m. the same day as her death. Paris had another wish honored, and that was to have her ashes scattered on water. She said she wanted her ashes scattered in the sea off South Padre Island, a sandbank resort off the coast of Texas in the Gulf of Mexico. South Padre Island had been a vacation spot several times over the years, and the girls had so much fun there and many happy memories. The family scattered her ashes forty-eight hours after her death.

Paris had made several requests to me: there was to be no funeral, only a memorial service, and she wanted it at her school. And she gave the details of that also.

Chapter 27

SIX WEEKS TO THE MEMORIAL SERVICE

aris wanted her memorial service to be held at her school and not a church. This I could understand as school and learning were her greatest joys outside of her love for Helen. I met with the principal, who gave permission for the service to be held in the gymnasium, which had a stage. The date was set for March 24, 2001. This was six weeks after Paris's passing.

During those six weeks I didn't know which end was up. I would walk around the house aimlessly. I would pick things up and lay them down again, not knowing why. I would go into a room to get something and forget what I was looking for. Thankfully I didn't need to worry about grocery shopping or cooking as friends and neighbors kept us well supplied with casseroles; my refrigerator and freezer were packed.

Paris had made it clear to me in those last days how she wanted things to be. She wanted her bedroom changed, and she wanted her bed moved out, and we did so after we retuned from scattering her ashes on South Padre Island. She wanted "Circle of Life," from *The Lion King*, to be played "and play it loud, Mummy." Also, "Truly Madly Deeply, I Want to Stand with You on a Mountain" by Savage Garden. "Tell everybody to listen to the words." Paris wanted all her friends to be dressed in "happy colors."

With the help of Sue, we created a memorial announcement. It included a verse Paris had written to me and slipped under my bedroom door eight weeks before she died.

We chose a picture of Paris that was my least favorite, but Paris had pasted it on the back cover of a little book that she was writing, she being the author, so I agreed to that. Just a little announcement, but it took every bit of my energy.

During this time, my own health was getting steadily worse. I could not lift my arms above my shoulders and the pain going through my body was agonizing. I had toothaches in all of my teeth as well as earaches in both ears. It was painful to bathe as the touch of the water on my skin made me wince. I was a mess. The dentist found no reason for the toothache and there was no infection in my ears. It got to the point that I did not want to share anything with anyone, because I thought I was going out of my mind. Very little made sense to me, and I had no one to talk to about it.

Losing Paris was only a part of my grief; my greater agony was knowing that I had survived her. My cancer was removed and I lived while she died. The guilt was slowly killing me. I didn't cry much during Paris's sixteen-month diagnosis, and not so much while she was fighting her cancer. I had accepted it and had to stay together to keep her going. Then I was too much in a state of shock over what happened the night of her death that the tears just didn't come. Almost as if the tears were stuck in me somewhere. My body was fast becoming crippled with pain, and I didn't know how to stop it. Every inch of my skin hurt, as if I were covered head to toe in severe burns. It hurt to stand, sit, or lie down. It hurt my scalp to wash or brush my hair. I'd look at my shabby appearance in the mirror and wonder who I was looking at. Who was that old woman in the mirror, and where did I go?

Chapter 28

A MEMORIAL FOR
PARIS PARDUE ACREE

Walking into the school gymnasium was like walking into an Easter gathering—the hall was full of beautiful flowers, and it was packed with as many adults as children, all of whom were dressed in pastel colors, just as Paris had wanted. It was a beautiful tribute to a little girl.

At the end of the service, everyone went out into the schoolyard. All the children, over a hundred, were given a yellow helium balloon on a purple string with a small blank card on the end to write a message on for Paris. We all sang as we let go of over a hundred yellow balloons; the sky looked beautiful.

I stood at the main doorway to thank everyone for coming to my little girl's memorial. As each person shook my hand and gave me a hug, the pain of the contact was becoming excruciating. I thought if one more person touched me, I would scream with pain. I managed to leave, stating I was feeling unwell, and Sue and her husband drove me home. Helen stayed with her dad that evening. Once at home, my agony intensified. It hurt to sit and it hurt to stand, and the toothaches and earaches had my head pounding; I could not escape the physical pain I was in.

I did manage to sit down on the couch and just went with the pain until I became numb. I sat there listening to the clock on the mantle ticking away. The constant ticking was annoying. Didn't the clock know that something awful had happened? How could it just go on ticking? The

Westminster chime struck ten. *That's right, just strike out your merry little tune while a person, a child, my child, is no longer here—because she is dead. Keep chiming away as if nothing has happened.*

All I wanted to do was to lie down. I felt exhausted, and it was a struggle to get my pain-riddled body off the couch. I rolled myself onto the floor and crawled on my hands and knees to my bedroom just a few feet away. As I got to the edge of my bed, I managed to pull myself up, flip on the light switch on the wall, then remove some of my clothes; it was just too painful to remove them all. It didn't matter. Nothing mattered anymore. I pulled back the bed covers and gently lowered myself onto the bed. Positioning myself was an effort, but once I was lying down I felt a little better.

I had forgotten to turn the light off. I just lay there knowing I hadn't the strength or energy to get off the bed again. That was the straw that broke the camel's back.

Chapter 29

"I" SAW MY BODY LYING
ON THE BED

I looked up at the cursed light on the ceiling; there it shone in my eyes, ensuring I would get no sleep. I lost it, just lost it, screaming up at the ceiling, at God.

Damn you! You took my baby! You stood by and watched as I was molested by the father you gave me! You stood by and watched as I was treated like dirt by the mother you gave me! You stood by while my heartbroken brother took his life! And you stood by and did nothing while my husband lied at the altar! What kind of god are you? What more do you want from me? Where have you been all of my life? You are merciless! Damn you! Damn you! I said, "Give me the cancer and save my baby." Oh, yes, you gave me the cancer all right, but you still took my baby, and now you leave me with the guilt! I swear you take my life this night, or I will take it myself!

My tirade to God had taken the last of my energy, and I couldn't move. I looked up at the cursed light and suddenly I saw, although didn't feel, my left hand moving upward. I looked a little to the right and saw my right had moving upward also, almost as if I were a marionette and my arms were being pulled by an invisible puppeteer. I tried to bring my arms down but couldn't. Then I was in total darkness and felt myself moving at a great speed, being pulled first to the right and then up over the top of my bed to the other side, where it was bright again, and I found myself in a slight kneeling position up off the floor, facing the nightstand and the wall.

Looking over at the bed, I saw my body lying there, separate from me. Yet somehow I felt peaceful, with no sense at all of surprise. Suddenly I could sense speed generating inside of me, and I flew backward, right through the bathroom door, going through the vanity cabinet. I could actually see the bottle of lotion that I had been looking for lying down behind a small cardboard box. I went through the walls of another room until I was in the hallway. I was in a more upright position, but not standing on the floor. Paris's bedroom door, at the end of the hallway, was open, and the room was so full of the brightest light. As I moved closer, I could see inside the room and there was my Paris, and behind her stood a man who looked like her father. As I moved along the hallway toward Paris, she said to me, without words, without moving her lips: "Are you ready?"

I answered her, without words: "Yes, I am."

Paris was older than the ten years and three months that she would have been. She looked as if she were in her early twenties. She was glowing, and her face was beautiful, her shiny brown hair still in the same bobbed style that she always wore. I moved into the room, and we put our arms around each other's waists and sped upward at about a thirty-degree angle, but we didn't go through any of the walls of the room or the ceiling.

In a split second we were coming out of a slight mist and moving off a lush green hill into a beautiful grassy, green meadow. It was almost as if every blade of grass was perfectly shaped. There was a melodious sound that was part of a greater silence. The sound was a part of me, as if I too were the melody.

Paris and I moved side-by-side along a pathway that at first appeared wet, but it wasn't—it was more like shiny concrete. To describe the scene around us as a beautiful meadow would be quite an understatement—it was that, but it was so much more. I could feel the lives of the many trees as if they were a part of me, or I a part of them. There were flowers everywhere, and the yellow ones stood out the most. We glided along the curvy pathway, moving without actually walking, and came to the left side of a very long building. The building was almost white and it sparkled in the light like granite. The side of the building was quite long and had built-in columns all along it. I didn't see any windows.

There were hundreds, possibly thousands, of other persons there, and I knew that they were gathered for my arrival. I was aware, somewhere deep within me, that they were my family, my bloodline, friends, and countless others that I had met during my earthly life. The oceans of others went back and back farther still, as if there was no horizon. The feeling of love emanating from them was in everything, and I was part of that love. This love was like swimming in the ocean, like being saturated. It felt normal, in many ways familiar, yet I had never experienced such an environment in this earth life.

The light around us was magnificent but not empty. What appeared to be a sky was a pale blue and pearlescent. Being with Paris was wonderful—it did not have a feeling of desperation or urgency or sadness or any of things I would have expected to feel on seeing her again. It was as if she was expecting me and I was expecting to be met by her.

She made reference to two things and asked if I would be willing to extend my stay in my earth life to fulfill these two opportunities. The knowledge of the nature of these "things" was not something that I could hold on to but would be made known to me later. At the time, I understood her admonition, but it was an understanding deep within me and not communicated in words.

She told me, again without words, that if I wanted to, I could go back for these two things. I hesitated because I wanted to stay home with her, yet *I knew* that there were others in the earth life, people I knew and loved who struggled as I once did. I knew I would be more help to them by being back in my body than I would by staying in heaven. She said if I wanted to go back, it would be okay, and "I will wait for you!"

I chose to return to the confusion of my life on earth, with the intention to get, be, do, or have these two things yet to be known to me and then come back to her immediately after those things were accomplished. On deciding to return, I felt like I was choosing to leave home, the place where I was meant to be, to come back here again to finish something or get started and complete something that I was yet to do, or be, or had not finished doing. What were these two items?

Suddenly I was lying in my bed again with both my arms up in the air. I was cold, so cold to the point that it was painful. I tried to pull my arms down so that I could pull my bed covers up to get warm but I couldn't move them. I had no thoughts or recollection after this. I'm sure I fell asleep.

Chapter 30

IT WAS MY BIRTHDAY
ALL OVER AGAIN

I awakened to a new morning with my bedroom filled with sunlight. I was curled up and lying on my side, and I could see the clock on my nightstand; it was just after 10:00 a.m. I felt so good inside and giddy like a little child, and I started laughing for no apparent reason. I sat up slowly out of habit, only to realize that I had no pain in my body. The physical pain of the last months was gone. I pressed on my arms and legs and all my joints and felt no discomfort at all. The toothaches and earaches had vanished.

I was up out of my bed like a spring lamb! I felt fantastic! I had a full "Knowingness" of the night before and was in the bathroom like a shot to dig into my vanity cabinet to get that bottle of lotion that I had seen as I passed through the vanity cabinet. There it was, behind the cardboard box. I felt an intense sense of exhilaration like I had never felt before. I was just so happy! I found myself walking through my house and just enjoying all I saw. It felt so good to be alive!

I went into another bedroom of the house, and, as I was leaving the room, something came flying at my face! I darted backward so as not to be hit by it, but it quickly returned, so to speak, to the picture frame on the bookcase by the bedroom door. It was a picture of Paris's paternal grandparents on their wedding day. Paris's late grandfather, who died many years before Paris was born, and whom she had never met, was the person I had seen standing behind Paris in her bedroom the night before.

I laughed out loud; I would have thought that Paris would have been in the company of Nana, or my late brother, Benny. How wonderful to know that she had finally met her grandfather!

I got to the phone and called Paris's father to tell him of my experience and that his late father was there with Paris. Without my asking him, he said, "I believe you. That doesn't surprise me."

I was absolutely overjoyed! I got in the shower and enjoyed shampooing my hair—feeling the warm water on my skin was sheer luxury. For the first time in months I was able to raise my arms above my head to bathe and dress. I styled my hair and picked out a pretty dress to wear. What was the occasion? I was just so happy!

I called my pastor and left a message to please visit after church. I could not wait to tell him my good news! In the meantime I sat on our back porch and enjoyed looking around the yard. In the furthest corner of I saw something yellow. I thought that maybe some little flower seeds that the girls and I had planted might have grown up. I reached the corner and saw that the yellow that had caught my eye was in fact a deflated yellow balloon with a purple string on it and a small tag that read: "I love you." This was one of the one hundred yellow helium balloons that we had let go at the schoolyard the day before for Paris's memorial service. The schoolyard was about two miles away from our house as the crow flies.

I barely had time to process what I'd just seen when I heard the doorbell ring. I could not get the door opened fast enough to welcome three of the clergy from church. I was so excited to see them. They looked at me with amazement, as I had gone through a total transformation since the day before at the memorial service when they had expressed their concern for me.

I was standing in the living room in front of them, all excited, telling them that I had been with Paris, and on and on I went trying to describe the events of the night before the best I could, when they asked me to come and sit down.

"Victoria, you have been through a very rough time these past eighteen months, and we have watched you with great concern. Please allow our wives to come for you tomorrow and take you to see your doctor. Maybe you need something to help you sleep."

I was somewhat surprised at their comments, as I was feeling better than I ever had. I assured them that I was feeling perfectly well.

"You see, Victoria, it doesn't happen like that."

I hadn't considered that they might doubt my experience. Had I gone completely mad altogether? No, I was right! I couldn't deny what I had experienced. I know the brethren were coming from a place of love and concern. They thought I was just having a dream.

After a while, they left, and I sat down on the couch, where I had sat night before in such agony, and where I now sat in peace and comfort. I was aware of the mantle clock chiming its beautiful Westminster chime. I sat for a while listening to the silence after the chime; it was so peaceful. Had I lost my mind? What had happened?

I went into my bathroom and picked up the bottle of lotion that had been hidden for so long. *Who was it that saw the bottle of lotion behind the cardboard box in the vanity that had a closed door on it? Who was it that saw me lying in bed the night before?* I had so many questions, but the clergy had said, "It doesn't happen like that."

Suddenly my thoughts went back to Paris's admonition. I knew there were two things she urged me to get, or maybe to do, but for the life of me I could not remember what they were. I sat on the edge of the bathtub, clenching the bottle of lotion and trying desperately to recall Paris's transmission to me. How could I have forgotten so soon? She was waiting on me! Now I was getting anxious. How could I forget something so important and yet remember all of the small details in perfect clarity?

As the days passed, I shared my experience with several others from church; the response was always the same. All showed sympathy but suggested that the trauma of my loss and my poor health had caused my thoughts. I hadn't thought that others would respond in this way; I wasn't trying to convince them of anything but merely telling the facts. Because of these responses, I chose to keep my experience to myself.

I was struggling with the label of the "poor mother who tragically lost a child." While the sympathy was comforting in the beginning, it began to be detrimental as time when on. The whispers that I heard of "poor Victoria" were not what I wanted or needed. I didn't want people to think I had gone out of my mind. When I had considered the possibility that I *had* "gone out of my mind," that rang true in a way that is hard to explain. "I" *had* escaped the mind of Victoria for a while, and her body, for that matter. That begged the question, who was it that had escaped my mind? I realized that the "I" who met Paris in her bedroom, and traveled beyond with her, and the mind of Victoria were not the same. Who was "I"?

Chapter 31

A KNOWING AWARENESS, A HIGHER STATE OF CONSCIOUSNESS, A SIXTH SENSE

I originally saw my out-of-body experience and connection with the eternal as a one-off event, an isolated occurrence. However, over time, I developed a greater realization, not in my mind, but through an additional sense, a sixth sense, that came through me. I often refer to this as a "Knowing Awareness," or higher state of consciousness. I use these phrases interchangeably.

I had the typical ups and downs of life over the next ten years as I tried to suppress my out-of-body experience. I was asleep, though sometimes aware of my sleepiness, and not accessing the sixth sense, or Knowingness that I acquired when I returned to my body.

We all know what our five senses are: sight, sound, touch, taste, and smell. These senses are all part of the human package. However, the sixth sense I talk about has its source not in the human brain but in the divine. This sense is not a function of mind or brain.

Previous to my out-of-body experience, and before Paris's diagnosis, my ability to discern my environment and relationships was comparable to a small, flat, one-inch-square mirror reflecting at me with some insight. In my self-imposed suffering at the guilt and loss of my daughter, I failed to access full discernment. Now, I experience this energy like a thousand of those small mirrors, like a multifaceted disco ball that reflects the light of insight in many directions simultaneously.

The most important awareness from this additional sense is that I am part of the oneness that we all are; while my body appears separate from others, I am fully aware that I AM that one in essence. I now Know, experientially, that "I" am that I AM.

I went through a period of self-imposed suffering as I tried to live fully in this world after having seen and experienced another, more perfect one. I became acutely aware of how everyone seemed asleep to the higher consciousness and absent of the sixth sense, but it was not for me to tell others that they were asleep. I know that we must each awaken to our own Knowing Awareness. This is not something that we can do for each other; we can only assist those who are ready by pointing the way.

Not wanting to be known as the "crazy lady" who had lost a child, I continued to keep my experience to myself. I know that in this regard I am not unique: many have lost children and people they love, and I don't claim that my pain was greater than theirs.

It was only in the eleventh year after Paris's passing that I felt to acknowledge openly, and to live from the higher self that I Knew I was, and to acknowledge that sixth sense. I took the risk of sharing by e-mail a brief synopsis of my experience with a dear friend whom I had not spoken to in many years. She was, and is, a spiritually attuned woman whom I've experienced as a soul sister.

As I clicked SEND, I realized that it was possible that she, like everyone else, might reject my message.

I waited to see if she would answer, though I didn't have to wait long: an answer from my friend showed up in my inbox the next day. I paused for a few minutes before I opened her e-mail, thinking how I would feel if she too thought I had gone crazy.

But I was shocked, in a good way, when my friend not only believed what I shared with her, but also made me aware that her son had had a similar experience many years ago and that he too was now being vocal about it.

This was a turning point for me. I had, until now, resigned myself to keeping my experience to myself, but my friend's belief allowed me to give myself permission to be vocal and share. For me there just came a point of openness, where I felt I needed to share—not for the purpose of bragging, but for being transparent. There is a higher purpose in the sharing, and it is sanctified by a divine source. This is the purpose of my return.

Chapter 32

THE TWO THINGS
WERE NOT FORGOTTEN

I t was further into the eleventh year after Paris's passing when those "two things" that Paris made reference to were made aware to me.

For eleven years I had been searching for a memory of the "two things" that I was supposed to do, be, or have—I could never quite recall Paris's inquiry. It turned out that I had been looking in the wrong place, because real Knowingness is never found in the mind. It comes from the source, that higher state of consciousness, or by use of the sixth sense, to access that which is the divine.

Suppressing my experience for so many years had created a blockage of a sort. I had allowed the disbelief and pity of others, and more especially my wrongful willingness to appease those who said that they loved me, to make me doubt my own awakening. Yet, in retrospect, I had many experiences with the Knowingness even during those years, as if to tell me to change course. At these times I was busy trying to fit in with the ways of the sleeping world of others, and struggling to do so. In all that time spent going after what the world encouraged, I only experienced additional suffering.

My wake-up call came in July 2012 at about 10:30 p.m., when I had a profound experience while listening to a recording of a radio broadcast online. The caller, a near-death experience researcher and author on the subject, said that those who have near-death experiences often have been given the choice to come back into their bodies, and while their admonition was never told to them directly, the experiencer would eventually become aware of it on his or her own.

As I listened to the broadcast and the revelation that the researcher shared, it was suddenly as if I had a covering or box over my head and everything was dark except for a couple of holes that I could see out of. I felt very light, yet my heart was racing. In front of my eyes appeared two words flashing like neon lights: *Faith. Enlightenment.*

I felt tears roll down my face at this. I Knew instantly, through Knowingness, that these were the "two things" that Paris had communicated to me in that glorious realm beyond the mist—they were my purpose in this earth life.

I found myself leaving the computer and going into my bedroom. I felt physically weak and just went to bed. I have no recollection of any thoughts or of going to sleep.

My next awareness was the motion of my own body sitting up in my bed in the dark and being quite shocked at being where I was.

"What am I doing back here?"

I spoke the words out loud. I looked around the room and saw that I was sitting up in my own bed, surrounded by my own bedroom furniture, in my own bedroom, in my own house.

"Where else would I expect to be"—I looked at the clock on my nightstand—"at 3:21 in the morning?"

I jumped up out of my bed and rushed with enthusiasm to my little home office. I squeezed through several packing boxes that would be loaded onto a moving truck the next week as I relocated to the Wasatch Mountains of Utah. I didn't quite know why I needed to move there, but I was following a strong inner prompting. I grabbed a yellow legal pad and a pen, rushed back to my bedroom, and jumped on my bed like a giddy teenager. It was there, with a feeling of great enthusiasm and excitement, that I began writing a list.

The list was of the many experiences I'd had with my late daughter, Paris, who had died of brain stem cancer at the age of ten, eleven years previously in 2001.

The list started with my own out-of-body experience after Paris's memorial service. Next on the list was the shared death experience with her upon her death. My pen kept going, and the list continued with the many things that Paris had shared with me, including telling me that I had breast cancer just two weeks after she was diagnosed with an astrocytoma in her brain stem.

This list read like a shopping list or a to-do list. Sometimes an entry was a single word or a short phrase. I sat and looked at the list that seemed to flow out of my pen; then the flow continued going back further, more words and phrases, all the way back to the day I realized I was pregnant with her. Tired and weary, and with little to no thought at all, I lay down and went back to sleep.

It was midmorning and I was awake again, sitting up in bed when I saw the yellow legal pad lying on the bed beside me. I recalled writing the list during the night. I sat for a while just looking at the list. Instantly, I felt a big smile on my face, and I began to laugh out loud; bursts of smiling and laughing out loud had become regular experiences for me since acquiring an almost continued Knowingness since my return from my out of body experience. I knew in that instant that the list I was looking at were the chapter titles of a book—this book.

MY PERSONAL PATH

I pondered in meditation how I might confer to others the access to and the use of divine inheritance, or higher consciousness. The following, with scriptural references, is what comes to me and may be best understood by those who embrace the cannons of the Bible. The sources I reference come from the New King James Version (NKJV) of the Bible.

For persons who describe themselves as agnostic or atheist, the process is the same. The names of deity may be replaced with source energy; we all have access to this higher frequency, no matter the labels ascribed or omitted.

Also, such teachings, presented from a different point of view, can be found in the *Tao Te Ching*, a work that was produced by Lao-tzu (551–479 BC).

This is for your consideration:

Luke 16:13 "No servant can serve two masters; for either he will hate the one and love the other, or else he will be loyal to the one and despise the other. You cannot serve God and mammon."

This is talking of the basis from which we live our lives: love or fear. We cannot have one foot in each. Choose one—I'm hoping it will be love. Love is the divine or source. Love is the higher consciousness.

Luke 9:62 "But Jesus said to him, "No one, having put his hand to the plow, and looking back, is fit for the kingdom of God.""

Having a work to do, do not look to the past. "Peace" is the fitness of the kingdom of God.

Mark 6:34 "Therefore do not worry about tomorrow, for tomorrow will worry about its own things. Sufficient for the day *is* its own trouble."

We are not to look back to the past and not to look to the future. We are being asked to look to the ever-present Now. The divine is only every-accessible in the Now.

Mark 12:22 "And whenever you stand praying, if you have anything against anyone, forgive him, that your Father in heaven may also forgive you your trespasses."

There is a prerequisite to experiencing the kingdom within: forgiveness. Without forgiveness it is unlikely that divine communion will be experienced. Likewise, holding a grudge will not afford the experience of a state of higher consciousness

Where are we, and how are we to access the Divine?

Luke 17:21 "Nor will they say, 'See here!' or 'See there!' For indeed, the kingdom of God is within you."

It is made very clear where this kingdom of God is to be found! Within you!

Psalm 46:10 Be still, and know that I am God; I will be exalted among the nations, I will be exalted in the earth!

John 14:20 "At that day you will know that I am in My Father, and you in Me, and I in you."

Be still in meditation for twenty to sixty minutes twice a day and truly Know God, experience God, the divine (the source).

It is my personal experience that in such a state of meditation, my body has no appetites; it will no longer hunger or thirst. This will bring about a natural fasting of my body. In other words, fasting is not something that I "do," but it is a natural by-product of being in divine communion.

Matthew 31–34 Therefore do not worry, saying, 'What shall we eat?' or 'What shall we drink?' or 'What shall we wear?'
For after all these things the Gentiles seek. For your heavenly Father knows that you need all these things
But seek first the kingdom of God and His righteousness, and all these things shall be added to you.

Therefore do not worry about tomorrow, for tomorrow will worry about its own things. Sufficient for the day is its own trouble.

In the stillness of the medative state of Being, possibly with the assistance of a mantra, the kingdom of God (divine communion) or the source, will be experienced, and his ways, or the ways of the source, will be Known to us. It is in the letting go of worry for the things that we seek that those same things maybe experienced, as God, or the source, already knows the desires of our hearts. We are limitless beings, nothing is ever withheld from us (and "all these things shall be added unto you").

Philippians 4:7 "And the peace of God, which surpasses all understanding, will guard your hearts and minds through Christ Jesus."

Following the admonitions of Jesus, or Lao-tzu, who says the same in the *Tao Te Ching*, we can experience a peace that is rarely understood by many. If I can Know this peace, experientially, then I know that anyone can.

John 14:27 "Peace I leave with you, my peace I give unto you: not as the world giveth, give I unto you. Let not your heart be troubled, neither let it be afraid."

It was always intended that we should live a life free of a troubled heart, yet we struggle and hold grudges from the past and worry about the future, and therein lies a state of deep depression rooted in judgment, which is rooted in fear.

I no longer live in fear. The love that I now experience allows me to live in peace.

I, as will others, have events and circumstances that come into our awareness. These are necessary for our evolution; they are the raw materials of the creative process. Some call these events "problems," which is a very negative word, with a negative energy. I choose to call these same circumstances "projects." Projects are positive and have a more positive energy. I love working on projects, and, by doing so, I create, and learning is the by-product of these creations.

EPILOGUE

My book assignment is now complete. The "list" that was given to me that July night in 2012, at 3:21 a.m., is now written, and even more items made their way onto the list in the end than were given to me that night. It is my hope that Paris will approve of what I've written. At the very least, she'll know that I did pay attention.

It is now 2013, and I currently live facing the beautiful Wasatch Front, a range of the Rocky Mountains in the United States. My move to Utah, just nine days after my "list" experience, was guided by inspiration. Keeping only what I needed, I gave away most of my household belongings to the Salvation Army, and loaded a moving truck and drove fourteen hundred miles from Texas. Here in Utah is where the book was written.

I have learned much over the years about the nature of human consciousness. There are many levels of consciousness, with their associated realities, and the level that each of us maintains is dependent on our perspectives and attitudes. The higher levels are phenomena that few will realize in their lifetimes.

I find myself giggling the way that Paris used to. She was right when she said that it was not she that was laughing; it is an energy that would take another book to explain.

The greatest plight, the greatest disease, of mankind is the belief that we are only bodies with minds and our way to happiness is to be found outside ourselves. In truth, there is another dimension to be experienced, in fact, a multitude of dimensions, and once you've experienced it, you realize what a sleepy, dream state our earth lives are really in.

While I use the word *Heaven* in the book title, it is for the purpose of using words with which the reader will be familiar; the truth is, heaven is an experience of spiritual awareness. It is an energy, and has a unique, heavenly reality where other beings and the divine, or source, is to be experienced. As we fluctuate in spiritual maturity, different realities will be experienced.

Being in a negative mind-set, as I was throughout Paris's illness, and especially the evening that I saw my body on the bed, I experienced greater pain. In this state, I created hell on earth for myself.

The most perfect way I can conclude my sharing is to refer to scripture and the story of the prodigal son (Luke 15:11–32 NKJV). I could recognize myself as a prodigal daughter. Yes, I came into this life with a great inheritance, but I was ignorant of my gifts and talents. *"I will arise and go to my father"* (v. 18). I wanted to escape the pain on this life, as I screamed at God to take me that night. *"But when he came to himself..."* (v. 17). I "came to myself" as I looked upon my body in the bed. *"And he arose and came to his father* (v. 20). It was my spirit leaving my body. *"But when he was still a great way off, his father saw him and had compassion, and ran and fell on his neck and kissed him."* Paris, in her divinity, came to meet me and escorted me home. God did hear my prayers, all of them, and my tirade, yet he offered me great compassion. *"And the son said to him, 'Father, I have sinned against heaven and in your sight, and am no longer worthy to be called your son.'"*(v. 21). I had lost my faith and cursed deity. *"But the father said . . . 'for this my son was dead and is alive again; he was lost and is found'. . . "And bring the fatted calf here . . ."* (vv. 22, 24 then 23).

Yes, I was very lost, spiritually hungry; now I am found. The spirit that I truly am was well fed on my "trip" beyond, and I continue to be fed ongoing, through the sixth sense. I am grateful to have another chance, to return to this mortal life, and to share. Now I am very aware of, and experience, my Divine Inheritance.

We may liken ourselves to the prodigal son or daughter, but we all have the same Divine Inheritance. This is not just a concept, but a realization, something to be lived, Now.

I Know that we are all of one essence; there is no spiritual umbilical cord that was cut. We come into this world worthy to allow for the Divine essence to have expression through us; we cannot fail to be worthy of that which we are. We have nothing to fear and our existence has no end, even while the human form may wither away. We are the eternal.

Many people are afraid of death. Our society tends to cringe at the very sound of the word. Many will experience the death of the body. Death is not the opposite of life; it is the opposite of birth. Life is eternal.

I enjoy my time working as a volunteer with hospice patients and bringing a message of comfort to them. Spending time with people who are soon to pass is a blessed experience for me, and witnesses to me what I already Know: only the human form dies, while the essence, or the spiritual beingness, of our loved ones lives on. In Knowing Awareness, I enjoy Paris in another way. She often said that she was a teacher, and she continues to be so; now I pay attention.

Life is a joy with only two important events worth mentioning, the first breath and the last breath; in between those two breaths is a divinely creative experience to be enjoyed.

Appendix

IN HONOR OF PARIS

$\mathcal{S}$everal verses have been written in honor of Paris.

Pam Kilman was a teacher at Paris's school. While Paris was never her student, Mrs. Kilman was touched by Paris, as were many adults. She wrote the following verse in Paris's honor and read it at her memorial service.

TIME FOR PARIS
By Pam Kilman
February 15, 2000

Time after time, I sat down to make a rhyme
So that you would know my views before we ran out of time.
I don't suppose a child could know why my struggle was with words.
Unless, of course, her struggles made some of mine look quite absurd.
Paris, I know you're still able to inspire a bit of prose.
I've watched you now with interest and you've made me contemplate
Why the lessons that your teachers learned were a child's to demonstrate.
I learned that life can be well-lived, 'though the future isn't bright.
You lived the brightest life you could. It seemed you had no fright.
We witnessed so much courage and acceptance in your fight.
All of us have marveled that you filled up many days
Acting "normally" and clinging to your childlike ways.
You did school work with classmates and laughed at all their jokes.
The amazing thing to me is that *you* offered *us* great hope.

The happy thoughts you brought to life are the things that we should note.
Harry Potter, your companion, became a friend of note.
J. K. Rowling helped define death with one of her book quotes.
I know that many people read her words and postulate
The imaginary world that she was able to create.
Your spirit makes a journey now that the living still debate.
I congratulate your family for their compassionate care.
I find it awe inspiring to know the burden you all shared.
They celebrate your living as they hold you in their hearts.
I know how often you encouraged them that death was just a part
Of the happy life you've shared with them from the very start.
Helen, Paris is with you in spite of the loneliness you'll feel;
Even when the things in your life seem to be going very well.
I know your life is blessed by a special "Sister's Bond."
I assure you that you're a tribute to the other one.
Please remember how much Paris wants your happiness to come.
We've admired your work to display smiles and take a skipping step.
Paris's inner strength and beauty is reflected in yourself.
Don't be afraid to get support if it's something you could use.
You've been such a supportive sister when it was very hard to do.
Mom and Dad, I cannot guess how painful this must be.
You've done your best for all this time to help Paris to feel free
To laugh like other children and be all that she could be.
We hope that you are not too numb to begin to recognize
How much the other people see the love that's in your eyes.
We gather now to celebrate a life that touched us all.
We all smile when we remember; whether we are small or tall.
Little Buddy, Sarah, made her heart-felt valentine.
Sheila Thomas with the bracelet that will represent in mind
The awesome kid who offered it with love for all of time.
I recognize young people who gathered by her side
With offers of true friendship to help her focus on the pride
Vertical Team Members foster with great teachers as their guides.
Relationships are life's treasures that will not be set aside.
You were all that kind of friend to Paris. It cannot be denied!
Now, Paris, I hope you have knowledge of these words that seem to flow.
I couldn't seem to say them to your face, ya' know?
You are an inspiration like the greatest of the great!
All of us who are left living are glad to celebrate
The precious love in living that we witnessed in you of late.

This was a special tribute offered by Marjorie Bell, one of Paris's teachers.

WHAT IS SUCCESS?
Attributed to Ralph Waldo Emerson

To laugh often and much;
To win the respect of intelligent people
and the affection of children;
To earn the appreciation of honest critics
and endure the betrayal of false friends:
To appreciate beauty;
To find the best in others;
To leave the world a bit better, whether by
a healthy child, a garden patch
or a redeemed social condition;
To know even one life has breathed
easier because you lived;
This is to have succeeded.

The journal entry that Paris had written in December of 2000, two months before she died. It reads:

December 11, 2000

> How I love you, I can't explain.
> I'm like a rose, already bloomed
> and ready to sing.
> Though I love you, I have to go.
> Heavenly Father is calling
> me home.

By Paris P. Acree
   To Mummy

As I reread the second line, "already bloomed" I realized that Paris was not sad to be leaving, as I read further it sounds a little apologetic at "I have to go," almost as if she realized her "mission" here was now complete.

I love you too, Paris! Thank you for coming into my life and sharing as you did. Thank you too for escorting me home to see and experience the things you were already so wise about. You are a wonderful teacher. I know you will continue to wait for me while I finish up my 'two things'." See you soon.

Love,
   Mum XXX

ABOUT *the* AUTHOR

*V*ictoria Mason Acree is an author, mentor, and inspirational speaker in the human potential and development arena. She enjoys giving seminars and accepting invitations as a guest speaker to the audiences of top events.

In 2013, Victoria was invited to be a contributing author, along with #1 *New York Times* bestselling author Jack Canfield, of the "Chicken Soup for the Soul" series, in the publication *Achieve–Conversations with Top Achievers*. In this book, Victoria shares with her readers her wisdom and expertise on how she has come to the top of her game despite personal tragedies.

As a returning guest on the radio airwaves, Victoria has shared her personal story, which has brought about many inquiries from listeners who want to know more about who and what they are, and she has responded to those inquiries and continues to bring hope to others.

Her presentations to the International Association of Near-Death Studies brought about many questions from her audiences that she was willing to answer.

Victoria graduated from Concordia University, majoring in business. Her love of numbers in tax preparation for a charitable organization was recognized by the Inland Revenue Service for her outstanding public service contribution to her community. Victoria has held membership in the Texas Society of Certified Public Accountants, and she is a Life Member of the National Association of Professional Women. She has started three businesses and was included in the 2010–2011 edition of the *Cambridge Who's Who registry of Executives, Professionals and Entrepreneurs*.

Having been a casual mentor to many for almost a decade, Victoria gave up her career in the financial industry, and obtained certification as a Business & Life Coach from Fowler Wainwright International Institute of Professional Coaching. Mentoring, and coaching by her personalized enlightened method, is her passion and purpose.

Victoria is a native of Scotland. Having visited many counties in Europe and living in Japan for a time, she emigrated to the United States in 1989. She currently resides in the Rocky Mountains in the United States.

Victoria is the president of her own business and mentor practice, Voice of Victoria LLC.

Victoria would love to hear how this book has inspired you! Contact her at victoria@voiceofvictoria.com or visit her website: www.voiceofvictoria.com